Oceanic Mind

The Deeper Meditation Training Course

By Tom Von Deck

Monkey Wisdom Meditation and Workplace Stress Management

www.DeeperMeditation.net

Front cover art by Amaloba

Interior and back cover art by Katie Rose Nelson (minus censor bubbles)

Order paperback copies and the audio course at www.DeeperMeditation.net.

Order the Deeper Meditation Audio Course and receive a free copy of the book shipped to you anywhere in the world.

And tell all your friends that they can take this course by visiting www.DeeperMeditation.net.

Table of Contents

Toasts

Pour yourself a glass of wine or juice for this.

A toast to the late Ann Martin, a healing arts teacher from Prescott who always knew how to listen to "Creator". To Arthur, the mime teacher who sees the value of physical training in the theater arts. To Dr. Munz, the philosophy professor who provided me with many tools to use my intellect properly. One cannot "transcend" the intellect until one understands it and learns how to use it properly and skillfully. To William Martino, a former monk, Kung Fu master and meditation master who is a pioneer of integrative approaches to meditation training. To Phyllis, a Hatha Yoga teacher who really knew what she was doing. To Swami Vidyadhishananda, who taught me Kriya Yoga. To Mark and Maya, good friends and fully devoted seekers and teachers (give me a ring). To Swami Paramahamsa Prajnanananda who showed me what the unhindered divine presence in a human being actually looks like. To Bill, a high school Latin teacher and former priest who led his classes in meditation every Friday. To Richard, a devoted Bhakta. To the Boulder Kirtan, where I learned many many devotional songs. To Neem Karoli Baba, who showed me Samadhi long after his earthly passing. To my dad and stepmom, John and Fay, two devoted seekers who answer the call of service. To my mom and stepdad, Paula and Art, two highly devoted seekers of Jesus... I'm getting kind of tipsy. Let's wrap this up... To the Most High, whoever that is, and all its manifestations or children, depending on how one sees it. To atheists, who challenge our mistaken symbolic representations of reality (and hopefully their own as well). For all the atheists reading this book... to Nothing! It brings great joy to say that.

Introduction to the Integrative Tuning Approach

The meditation manual which you are about to read may be considered "unique" by many people. This work revolves around the "Integrative Tuning" (IT) approach to meditation training, sometimes known as "Monkey fusion" depending on mood. In IT, we are tuning ourselves on every level of being in preparation for deep meditation. This is not a specific technique being taught here. You will definitely learn some techniques in this program. However, IT is an "approach" that is compatible with all spiritual and stress reduction techniques. Therefore, IT is for the beginning student of meditation/Yoga who wishes to learn a technique as well as the advanced student who has already found a compatible practice.

The process of IT begins with the "7+1 Tuning Method", a personalized warm up program which works with all aspects of one's "matter and energy" - muscles, energy, nature, intellect, imagination, emotions and breath – from gross (physical) to fine (internal activity and breath). The "+1" refers to Spirit, i.e. the stillness behind all energy and form. The exercise associated with Spirit is the meditation itself.

Tuning yourself for deep meditation does not strictly involve warm up workouts just prior to meditation. IT offers a complete method of integrating both this tuning process and meditation into everyday activity for a profound momentum of peace on even the most hectic time schedule.

IT is neither secular nor religious. However, IT is as secular or religious as the individual who practices this strategy. The author uses the words "spirit", "God" and "soul" in this book. You do not need to do the same. These words are individual preferences.

In this book, you will learn a structured approach to IT. However, as your intuition develops, the approach may be altered according to your own intuitive wisdom. Everyone's intuition will guide them in unique ways.

Just because IT has a neat sounding name, that does not make the approach a new invention. All the material has been around for thousands of years. Furthermore, there are other teachers who present similar approaches, to one degree or another, for entering deep states of inner communion. Despite this, IT and similar approaches are still rare in meditation and Yoga training.

One of the reasons for the rarity of IT type approaches is that every lineage, technique and school of thought has its own "pet" set of techniques, ways of teaching, emphasis and warm up exercises (if any). In this age, such protectionism is quickly changing, however.

When we can break through the factionalism, we are then able to see commonalities between traditions. Once we accomplish that, along with regularly plunging into the ocean of consciousness over a long period, we can then extract the gems from each faction and integrate them in new and profound ways.

Such is true for the myriad forms within Qigong (aka Chi Gong, Chi Kung or Taoist Yoga), healing arts, different religions as well as spiritual and stress reduction disciplines of all kinds.

The purpose of this book is not to knock down factionalism. Some people find it necessary to protect the purity of a particular teaching for future generations of people who connect with that teaching. There is a lot of merit to that.

There are others who practice specific techniques for years and years. They teach what they are most comfortable with. There is much nobility in this.

Another group of people are devoted to factionalism. They are following a tendency of the human ego which desires to overpower other identities with its own sense of identity. Fundamentalism is a prime example of this. The fundamentalist creates an identity through symbols or a practice that he/she is already used to and then attempts to ensure that his/her/their symbols reign supreme. It is the conqueror's approach. A fundamentalist has a hard time seeing the reality beyond their symbols (e.g. a redheaded Irishman named Jesus vs. the reality of pure consciousness). Such a tendency is less noble than the protection of purity of a particular teaching. See the "Symbolitus" section for more on this topic.

Another reason for the relative uniqueness of this text is that most practices do not include work that is specifically directed toward all levels of being – intellect, body, emotions, energy, the "stillness" beyond energy and form, imagination, etc. All effective practices ultimately work on all these levels. However, they don't necessarily do so directly with conscious intent from the start.

Most traditions do have warm up strategies to prepare the mind and body for meditation. They also typically have prescriptions for integrating meditation into daily Life. Some prescribe ways to "project" or to share your cultivated meditative peace with the rest of the world, such as in the healing and shamanic practices in Qigong. Oceanic Mind provides you with the resources to develop the strategies and techniques that you are most compatible with so that you resonate with every aspect of your meditation and mind body training program.

IT is merely an indicator that the world is becoming smaller. Think about this. Factionalism was much easier when there were a billion people (or a few million) on Earth with no telephones, airplanes or internet. Now, we're forced to get to know each other a little better.

If you wish to help this project, then there are some things that you can do. You can tell all of your friends that they can find this training course at www.DeeperMeditation.net. The first 100 out of 193 pages are free in pdf format. Donations for the rest of the book can be sent via Paypal for the rest of the book. You can also tell them, of course, that paperbacks, The Deeper Meditation Audio Course and employee meditation seminars and products for workplaces are available. If one honestly cannot afford these training materials, they can contact the author. No one will be locked out for lack of funds.

Such an approach is much better than the common method of providing you with watered down "teaser" garbage, then asking you to sign up for the "full course" for $249.95. These are the times to really heal ourselves for the collective good. We should not be locked out of this process because of a lack of funds. Such mentalities invite pirates, probably for good reason.

I'm sounding a little feisty toward folks who tease people and hold their teachings ransom. Keep in mind that the goal of meditation is not to become passive and apparently "nice" from an intellectually conceived perspective. Meditation allows you to become a clearer and clearer vessel of the Supreme Love. The

Supreme Love does not necessarily enlist passive vessels to do its work. Love comes from within the deepest self rather than from an intellectual concept of "being nice". Love is not necessarily "nice" in the usual sense. Think of the Goddess Kali. She wears the skulls of demons around her neck. Behind her ferocious appearance is the face of pure love. Otherwise, she would not be the "Divine Mother".

Do not mistake this principle for an excuse to be mean to others. If feistiness truly comes from the heart, inner stillness, nonattachment and intuition, you will know it. Otherwise, "Be nice", whatever you think that means.

The intent here is not to tell you what to do. Your boss is not me. Your innermost self – your "still soft voice" - is your boss and your job is to develop the stillness of mind to listen to it on deeper and deeper levels until it becomes the only one worth listening to.

Anyway, I'm just kidding. I do understand the fear of not being able to make a living. The feisty talk is just to rattle some cages and make a few good points about what meditation is not. I was designed to work with all types of people – rich, poor and everyone else. It makes sense, then, that I would not keep people who lack funds out of the loop.

If you're relatively healthy and are not pregnant or menstruating, you may have no issues with any of the exercises in this book. However, if you are pregnant (or recently gave birth), menstruating *, or if you have blood pressure and asthma issues, then you may wish to avoid "hot" exercises that involve dynamic breathing and dynamic body movement.

It is best to consult a doctor before trying any of these exercises if you are unsure. The above mentioned health conditions (and blessings in one of those cases) are common in the list of contraindications for various mind-body training techniques. Two more that come to mind are Epilepsy and Diabetes.

Exercises discussed here without contraindications include very gentle self massage, soft flowing movement without strain, exercises from the Breathing Preliminaries section, singing, imagination and intellect exercises, sitting meditations and certain forms of gentle energy work. Again, if there is any question, even for these exercises, consult a good doctor. The reader must assume full responsibility for the results of the practices in this book. I've never had problems in the past 2+ decades of meditation practice, but I've always been fairly healthy. Epileptics should be cautious about all the exercises in this book.

It is recommended for prenatal and recently postnatal moms that they attend prenatal and postnatal Yoga classes. The teachers of such classes are well trained to keep your baby safe. Read this book anyway, however. It may greatly enhance any specific techniques that you choose.

Nothing in this book is claiming to cure or prevent any disease or to replace the advice of medical personnel. In other words, I am a puppet of the Food and Drug Administration. Hi Ho the Merry – O!

Another thing: For every mind-body training technique, there are many schools of thought. Be ready for people to tell you that you're doing it wrong. Welcome to the world of meditation!

If you receive any feedback about what you learned here, please send them my way. This book is a work in progress and feedback is welcome. There may be a few revisions of this book over time. Feedback from meditation teachers and students, doctors and healers is essential for this type of literature. If you personally have questions about the instructions in this book, please ask. The content may be changed accordingly for greater clarity. An email with a relevant subject line works best for this.

A little word about myself: I am an internationally available workplace meditation trainer, stress management speaker, spiritual speaker and author. I also create products for employee wellness programs such as the 400 minute long audio course.

The Deeper Meditation Audio Course features all the exercises in this book plus lots of information on making meditation a much easier and more customized process for people of all religions, temperaments and hectic time schedules. There is less spiritual terminology in the audio course and therefore less cultural distractions. There is also a more secular and wellness oriented edition of this book. A secular approach is often vital when working with a culturally diverse workforce. Visit DeeperMeditation.Net for info on any of these services.

The exercises in Oceanic Mind are carefully chosen for their ability to be transmitted through the written word. They are also thoroughly tested for "user friendly" qualities, so hopefully you'll find that the exercises are easy to follow and learn.

Enjoy,

Your friendly Monkey Wizard

Tom Von Deck

What is Meditation (and What the Hell is Yoga for that Matter)?

When a wave settles down, then it instantly
recognizes that its source in ocean - infinite,
silent, and unchanging - was always there.

-Deepak Chopra, M.D.

Meditation means to tap into the core of Being. Sounds trippy. We can speculate on this all we wish, perhaps at the nearest coffee shop. It only makes sense, however, when speculation gives way to pure experience. The words "tapping into the core of Being" did not precede Being. Being came first. Meditation is the bridge to understanding this concept from the depths of Being – beyond intellectual concepts.

We can liken our egos to the waves of the ocean. The waves are in constant motion and flux. The ocean beneath the waves, however, is deep and still. Meditation gradually allows us to experience ourselves as the ocean rather than just the waves. The experience of the oceanic mind has been described by yogis as "absolute existence, absolute consciousness and absolute bliss".

Do we really understand this concept? Do we now know the answer to life, the universe and everything? Not even close. This is all talk. Talk is always in symbolic form. Symbols can only inspire and lead us toward reality. When we confuse the symbols for the reality, we find ourselves in fights and quarrels over whose symbols are better.

Some people describe meditation as a digestive process of the mind. We accumulate experiences. When we don't "digest" these experiences properly, we get clogged up with indigestion. Our psychological/spiritual digestive system is just as important as our physical one.

To present meditation in another way, one can say that it is perception of perception. When we are fully conscious of our perception, we realize how full of crap we really are. The Big Joker in the sky honks our nose, sprays us in the face with a seltzer bottle, laughs maniacally and tells us how funny we were while repeatedly smacking us on the shoulder and continuing to laugh maniacally, dropping the cigar and choking on the smoke. Then, we pee our shorts in agreement and realize that the Big Joker was within us all along, laughing maniacally.

Maybe this isn't true, or maybe it is. If not, it's pretty close. Perhaps I'm full of crap. Ok, I'm definitely full of crap.

When we fully realize how full of crap we really are, extreme happiness, bliss and love results. That is because we've tapped into the source of all these things. This source goes beyond all conditioning and intellectual definitions of reality.

But don't ask me. Practice meditation and ask yourself.

All this talk about "going beyond intellectual concepts" may lead one to believe that meditation is a "right brain" activity. It is not. Meditation facilitates the integration of all parts of the brain; left/right, top/bottom, center/periphery. Neurons create more synapses (the connectors between brain cells) and impulses gradually travel around the brain and nervous system more efficiently and coherently. The suppression of the "left brain" can only lead to problems. Don't abandon the intellect. When the intellect is truly in sync with the rest of you, it becomes your best friend.

Yoga is derived from the Sanskrit word "yog" which literally means "yolk". The connotation is "union" – union with "God" (who?), union with our deepest self and the union of all parts of ourselves. Pantanjali, in the Yoga Sutras, described Yoga as "the cessation of the fluctuations of the mind". The more we meditate, the more we understand what he meant.

In the Bhagavad Gita, Krishna described Yoga as the spiritual path. Every yogic practice he mentioned is universal to the mystic path (the path of direct experience and realization) of every religion. Therefore, Yoga, in its purest sense, is not a set of Indian practices for better health, fitness and maybe some spirituality. Yoga is THE spiritual path. Just because the word is in Sanskrit, this does not mean that it must only be associated with cultures affiliated with Sanskrit. Only the symbols and emphases vary in the various cultural and individual manifestations of the one path – Yoga.

In the Bhagavad Gita, Krishna mentions Karma Yoga, one of the fundamental premises of the Bible's Book of Matthew. Karma Yoga involves selfless service without "blowing your trumpet". You are offering the credit to the one who gives you life. If you've stilled the mind to the point where the "still small voice" leads you, then Karma Yoga means to follow that voice without being attached to the fruits of your actions – reward or punishment. It all begins as "do good without bragging" and becomes more refined from there.

As you advance on the path to paradise, this teaching becomes even more refined. Never read a scripture and say "I get it". "Getting it" is a process. Stay on the path and, in 10 years, the spiritual readings you are looking at today will take on a whole different meaning.

In light of this, there is a reason why this book may seem to be "talking down" to you at times. We may, to some extent, "get" a spiritual truth such as "listen to your innermost self". However, do we truly "get it"? "You either get it or you don't" does not apply here. The unfolding of consciousness is a process. We should leave all or nothing thinking to fundamentalism.

We all think we're so enlightened, don't we? Align yourself even more with your truest self. Get it?

Anyway, Bhakti Yoga is the Yoga of devotion. In India, Bhaktas usually practice Bhakti through singing the "names of God". Some just meditate on God in one or another symbolic form until they transcend that symbolic form and see God directly. For example, If you meditate on a redheaded Irishman named Jesus (Jesus was never his name) long enough, you will gradually begin to see what people mean when they say the word "God" (who is not Irish. Well, not normally.). Bhakti is fundamental in every religion and spiritual path.

The path of meditation was another one mentioned by Krishna. Krishna said that this path is very very important.

Is Meditation Religious?

Meditators come from all religious backgrounds and some have no religious beliefs at all. There is no need for religious beliefs. In fact, the Buddha said not to believe anything until it is directly experienced. This expression was mistaken by many to be a call to atheism. He only said this because people became too caught up in symbolic representations of reality. In other words, they forgot the reality behind such nonsense words as God, Soul, etc. because they were too caught up in words and ideas.

Meditation is an experience that gradually transcends all symbolic belief. However, you may, while meditating, accidentally access the fundamental root of all religious belief systems and symbols. Meditation awakens our consciousness and soul perception (why did he just use those nonsense words again, Claudia?).

What do the terms consciousness and soul perception mean? Nothing until we experience such things directly. Until then, such thoughts are nothing but gibberish.

Keep meditating. The knowing process is cumulative, always unfolding until you "get it", decide that you know everything, then "get it" again, decide that you now finally know everything and then "get it" yet again.

To be fair, the talk about gibberish words is not exactly true. Don't believe everything this crazy author says. Spiritual concepts can be vehicles leading to the direct experience of the reality behind them if we use them correctly. The Yogis often meditate on a symbol or concept of God until the reality behind the concept is revealed to them through direct experience. The symbol (thought form), in this case, is used as a tuning device to "tune" into reality like a radio dial. It begins as an approximation of reality and expands from there. There is a positive role for symbols. Otherwise, this book would have no value.

If you're just looking for no-nonsense health and vitality rather than the mumbojumbo, then go for it. You'll find improved health and maybe you'll eventually begin to understand some of the mumbojumbo woowoo stuff.

One thing that can be said of the intellect is that it is only a fragment of your consciousness. Therefore, it will never truly understand the spiritual mumbojumbo, scripture or anything else. Understanding only occurs through the whole being. The intellect always tries to dominate and declare its knowledge superior. Don't believe it. Integrate the intellect with the rest of your being and declare that you don't know jack poop.

Oh, and be sure to declare your truth to the world. The world needs it.

Monkey Business

Before concluding this chapter, it may be nice to explain all this monkey business. Buddhists often compare the mind to a monkey (the monkey mind). Monkeys swing from tree to tree picking fruit off each one. One can say that monkeys are "all over the place". Such is the mind.

How do we tame the monkey? Do we beat it? Do we force it to be still? When we try to force the mind to be still, it will bombard us with even more thoughts. Some describe meditation as the absence of thought. Perhaps there is some truth to that. However, this is not the starting point. The mind is tamed with love and self compassion, not force.

When our monkeys are tamed, they become Hanuman (Hahn'-oo-mahn) – the monkey god of Hindu lore. Hanuman was single mindedly devoted to Ram (pronounced Rom), a king. Ram symbolized God and sometimes, more specifically, he symbolized God in the aspect of the deepest truth behind all our symbols and concepts. Hanuman is pure devotion. The tamed monkey becomes a tool leading us to the Unfathomable Ultimate Reality – something that can never be found through a coffee shop conversation or a book, but through direct experience over time as stillness of mind is cultivated.

Benefits of Meditation

Meditation allows us to condition ourselves to enter the essence of life itself. We're plunging into the center of it all. When we do this, all aspects of life receive the benefit. Therefore, the answer to the question "what are the benefits of meditation?" is "who cares?" If you need a list of all the aspects of life, you can Google "benefits of meditation" and you will receive a list of all aspects of life.

Preliminaries

Regularity and Consistency

Every book on meditation practice for beginners emphasizes the importance of a regular practice in a particular place (chair, couch, room, Zen garden, etc.) at a particular time of day. Pavlov's experiments with the salivating dogs and the bell confirmed what meditators have always known. If we associate our beds with sleeping, it may not be a good idea to meditate on our beds. Meditating on our beds can lead to drowsiness rather than the calm and alert state that meditation requires. However, if we associate a particular pillow, chair or time of day with meditation practice, then it becomes easier to enter a meditative state on that pillow, chair or during that time of day.

As for times of day to meditate, it is best to devote some time in the morning and some time at night. Sunrise is a wonderful time if you can handle waking up that early without harming the rest of your day. It is true that some folks have tight schedules. Consider every minute spent in meditation a time investment that improves every other activity, including sleep. If you can only do your practice in the morning or at night, then that is ok. Consistency is what is most important.

Another point to make about consistency is that it is better to meditate for one minute seven days per week than it is to meditate for seven minutes one day per week. It is the routine that is important.

That is not to say, however, that you must never skip a day. Just don't screw up your overall habit that you created. If you do, then you can gently recreate the habit without blaming yourself.

One day at a time. Yes, we're all addicts. That's why the AA motto works for everyone.

Speaking of "screwing up"... When you develop the good habits of consistent meditation practice, it is tempting to become overly attached to it. The mind may associate meditation with "good" and other activities as "not as good", creating a false dichotomy. This association can lead some people to forsake fun, parties, active engagement in the world, etc. Such an association is merely a concept that exists in our minds.

Our intuitive guidance may be whispering to us to go out and have fun at the '80's dance party rather than meditate. However, if we have the false dichotomy in our heads, then we will not listen to such guidance and our spiritual development will suffer.

During one period of intense practice, I was invited to a party. My intuition had been telling me for at least a year that I needed to party more often. I got a little drunk and exchanged good stories with 8-10 others. The next morning, when I woke up, I felt calm and clear like I spent the whole night meditating instead of partying. It was exactly what was needed. I continued to practice the following night.

The moral of the story is this. Do not succumb to asceticism. It is an addiction which can be as damaging as burgers and fries and general "sense slavery" as the yogis call it. Asceticism and "sense slavery" are two sides of the same coin. Avoid such extreme polar opposites. Develop stillness of mind, tap into your intuition and follow it. Then, allow your inner stillness and intuition to deepen over time and follow it some more. Repeat.

Do you believe the last paragraph? Pretty sound, right? You shouldn't believe it. Some people are called, by their innermost selves to become ascetics, at least for awhile. For these folks, asceticism is not a dangerous addiction. It is what these individuals need today for optimum growth in the long run or perhaps to properly dispense an important teaching to the right people.

We are taught by our social institutions that "outward" is the way to be. At some point on the path, we realize that we should be heeding the call to go inward. We must not get stuck in such a rebellious state and remain "inward" all the time, thinking that this is superior. Eventually, it becomes time to integrate the internal with the external. Hermithood may be an intermediary step in this direction for some people.

So, do not believe me when I make a generalization about what everyone needs, ok? Not everyone needs to avoid the ascetic lifestyle just as not everyone needs to become an ascetic. Align yourself with your deepest intuitive self and find out for yourself whether you are being called into hermithood.

This all leads us to another question. Does everyone need to align themselves with their deepest intuitive self? Align yourself with your deepest intuitive self and find out.

Did you see that one coming?

Avoid Spiritual Materialism

Chogyam Trungpa, the Tibetan Rinpoche who cofounded Naropa University (with Allen Ginsberg) and the Shambhala Center in Boulder, Colorado, spoke and wrote extensively about "spiritual materialism" – attachment to "spiritual phenomena" and to the "spiritual experience".

The false dichotomy of spiritual materialism is a concept that flows along the following lines. Visions, ecstatic trance, psychic phenomena, feelings of deep bliss, miraculous healings, etc EQUAL spiritual development. Furthermore, a lack of such wild experiences EQUALS a lack of "spirituality". This dichotomy causes people to chase after the so-called spiritual experience. Superiority trips sometimes occur if phenomena become frequent.

Phenomena **rise and fall** as you walk the path. If you're attached to it, it can only hinder you so that you become stuck, unable to walk further on the path. You're chasing after a sensation like an addict chasing after heroin. In other words, you're engaging in sense slavery. While meditating, if such extraordinary phenomena happen (and they will when the time is ripe), just **let them rise and fall** like your breath. Appreciate their special purpose in the moment. When you let go of your attachment to these things, then they will become more consistent anyway as your circuitry is gently opened and conditioned over time. If you remain attached, they will either become more elusive or bring you some powerful, perhaps unwelcome, lessons about attachment. **Let it all rise and fall like waves on the ocean**.

The main lesson here is to let go of expectations in your practice. The main reason that many people abandon their practice is that they have too many ideals and expectations about it. Attachment to the ideals brings disappointment and frustration. Give up such attachments and you will realize such ideals in due time. You are probably making progress without knowing it.

None of this means that developing psychic powers and the like is a bad thing. Eshu (Jesus) said "Seek the kingdom first". When you seek the kingdom, then the king will let you know if your next stage of development involves consciously developing such "siddhis" or "charisms". If not, then they may just unfold naturally as you go deeper into the kingdom – or not.

As a side note, it may be worth mentioning that Trungpa was from the "crazy wisdom" tradition. He was a master of meditation who was known for being able to outdrink anyone. A look into his eyes revealed total stillness. It is possible that he did not have any attachment to alcohol. It is the author's suspicion that he stepped out of the way of his innermost self which became his primary motivator.

When you have truly accomplished this surrendering process, you have permission to do whatever you wish without repercussion (Caution: Do not assume that you have accomplished this already after tasting some of God's power in meditation. There are too many destructive half-baked gurus out there who have made this assumption about themselves. It is best not to become one of them.). This is because you are acting exactly in accordance with Spirit's dictates, from the center of being. When you accomplish this, you will probably appear like a hypocrite according to other people's false belief systems of what "spiritual" means. When you stop caring about APPEARING to follow your principles, then you are one step closer to the perfection of Karma Yoga.

Some people thought that Trungpa was a crazy hypocrite. There's only one way to know whether that is true, and here's a hint. It is not through any idea of "spirituality" or of anything Trungpa said versus what he did. Perhaps Trungpa's shenanigans were tools for teaching people lessons about the false dichotomy of asceticism vs. sense slavery... or maybe he was a crazy hypocrite. In any case, "Spirituality" is one of the biggest nonsense words in history. It's a hoax, and a very devilish one at that.

Meditation and Food

When you begin your practice, make sure your last meal is at least half digested. This means it's better to wait at least three hours after your last meal before you begin your regular practice. The digestive system uses a lot of energy when processing food. Meditation becomes much harder during this process.

When eating, it is best to be mindful of the whole process – giving thanks for the food, biting, chewing, swallowing and reaching for more. The more mindfully you eat and the better you chew your food, the more nutrients you absorb from the food. A meditative state becomes more available if you practice eating mindfully.

Another point to consider is that yogis say that one should never eat until one is "full". It is best to stop when you are maybe two thirds full. Meditation becomes more natural when you follow this guideline.

And of course, healthy food is better than unhealthy food, as painful as it is to say it.

Momentum

Each act of consciousness development paves the road for the next. If you sit down to meditate and it feels fruitless - i.e. tongues of fire did not descend from the heavens, Jesus did not pay you a personal visit, you were not thrown into ecstatic flailing and flopping around the room, etc. – it is still fruitful. Your practice paved the way for a deeper practice next time around. You may have experienced profound healing without even knowing it. A lot more happens than meets the eye. Therefore, consistency in practice creates consistency of deep levels of consciousness through a cumulative effect.

The previous paragraph is a repeat of earlier information in this book. These points cannot be stressed often enough. Please read the previous paragraph five times in a row if the need arises. Ask a tattoo artist to, well, never mind.

The Five Minute Intertwine

The "five minute intertwine" is a great way to increase momentum in your practice. There are probably many times in the day when you are able to take two to five minutes to center your mind. Some of the warm-up exercises mentioned later in this book are perfect for this. You can disappear into the bathroom for some exercises or you can take five minutes to practice the "inner smile", mindful breathing or a mantra at your desk. Breathing into a stretch, shoulder rolls, self massage and pranayama exercises are great as intertwine practices.

The result of the intertwine is to ground meditative practice into everyday life as well as to create a cumulative momentum toward clear consciousness and deep healing. You may or may not be aware of all the immediate profound effects of the intertwine. However, when you get home from work, you will have more energy and a more peaceful mind. Such a state will help you to keep your regular meditation schedule and allow you to slip more deeply and readily into the oceanic depths. The oceanic depths, in turn, will also help you to integrate a wonderful state of mind into daily life through the intertwine. This, also in turn, will enhance your formal practice... and on and on. Again, there is more going on behind the scenes than you may realize.

By the way, just like most of the information in this book, the term "five minute intertwine" was not my invention. I learned about the intertwine from a former monk, William Martino, founder of The Flow Program, whom I studied with for a couple years. He calls it "interweaving" these days (this guy loves to develop new vocabulary for teaching purposes). You can use either term. It's the same stuff. Language is just a tool.

It's impossible to invent anything new in the "inner sciences". You can only fool people by coming up with new language, trademarks, teaching styles and such.

Posture

Standing Posture

1. *Stand with your feet shoulder width apart. Relax and allow gravity to pull you down with equal pressure on the center of both feet. Hands are at your sides.*

2. *Breathe evenly through your nose. Feel the breath initiating in the abdomen (see the Breathing Preliminaries section for a more refined technique. The refined technique is after this section in order to make you come back to this one. Devilish, yes.)*

3. *Allow your hips to sink. At the same time, lift up the chest a little bit while imagining your hips "opening". Relax into this posture. You are relaxing into a form rather than acting like a jellyfish. You are creating a route for Spirit to enter into form.*

4. *Sink into your center of gravity, the navel center. This is the point about two inches below the navel and about two inches in.*

5. *Tuck in your chin a little bit toward your throat and imagine a string pulling your head up from the baby soft*

spot at the top of the head. Let your vertebrae "stack" one by one from the bottom to the top.

6. *Smile at your third eye between the eyebrows. Smile at your jaw.*

7. *Pay attention to your relaxed jaw, your relaxed eyes, your relaxed hands, your center of gravity (2 inches below your navel and 2 inches in). Relax into your center of gravity. You can use the "tense and release" or "clench and release" methods to relax these parts.*

8. *If your spine needs more relaxing, you can try to stretch it out, one vertebra at a time, making yourself as tall as possible. Don't move your limbs. Stretch the vertebrae apart. Then, shrink and compress your vertebrae, making yourself as short as possible. Do this a few times and "stack" them again.*

9. *Stare straight ahead, neither squinting nor widening the eyes. Do not stare intently.*

10. *Defocus the eyes. Soften the gaze and the eyes, looking outward and inward at the same time. "Feel" inside the body while looking at nothing in particular. Be conscious of the whole field of consciousness.*

11. *Be conscious of everything without attraction and repulsion – i.e. clinging to comfort and pushing away discomfort. Be present with yourself and the environment.*

12. *Notice any inner sounds or frequencies you might hear.*

13. Be mindful of the Earth beneath your feet and the sky above you. Integrate this into steps 9-12.

14. Before meditation, place the bottom side of your tongue on your palate (roof of mouth). The tongue should point backwards toward your throat, the tip being as close to your throat as possible without strain. Your tongue, in this position, completes the energy circuit that travels up the back of your spine and down the front of your spine. It is essential for the downward route. When you're COMPLETELY relaxed (perhaps years down the road), your tongue will slip into your nasal cavity.

Sitting Posture on a Cushion

1. Sit and cross your legs. It is best if the knees are lower than your butt and pointing slightly downward if that is possible.

2. Plant your tailbone in a position that feels just right.

3. Let gravity pull you down while you lift your chest and mentally open the hips.

4. Tuck in your chin just a little bit toward your neck while imagining an invisible string pulling your head up from the baby soft spot at the top of your head. Stack the vertebrae from the bottom to the top.

5. Relax into this position. The back should be as straight as possible without much strain.

6. Rest your hands comfortably on your lap. If you wish, you can use the Gyan Mudra. In Gyan, your index finger and thumb are making a circle with the remaining

fingers as straight as possible but relaxed. The backs of your hands are resting comfortably on your lap, probably near your knees. Gyan creates an energy circuit that aids concentration.

7. *Smile at your third eye (between the eyebrows) and jaw, relaxing them. You can also "tense and release" and/or "clench and release" to relax them. Tense the hands and relax them.*

8. *If your spine needs more relaxing, you can try to stretch it out, one vertebra at a time, making yourself as tall as possible. Don't move your limbs. Stretch the vertebrae apart. Then, shrink and compress your vertebrae, making yourself as short as possible. Do this a few times and "stack" the vertebrae again.*

9. *Stare straight ahead with eyes neither squinting nor widened. Defocus the eyes. Soften the eyes and the gaze and look at nothing in particular. Be conscious of the environment while "feeling" inside the body. Be conscious of the whole field, internal and external, without attraction and repulsion – i.e. clinging to comfort and pushing away discomfort.*

10. *If your sitting meditation practice requires it, close your eyes or keep them 9/10 closed (to prevent melatonin from making you drowsy, the 9/10 method allows some light in).*

11. *Before meditation, place the bottom side of your tongue on palate (roof of mouth). The tongue should point backwards toward your throat, the tip being as close to your throat as possible without strain. Your tongue, in*

this position, completes the downward energy circuit that travels up the back of your spine and down the front of your spine. It is essential for the downward route. When you're COMPLETELY relaxed (perhaps years down the road), your tongue will slip into your nasal cavity.

Sitting Posture on a Chair

Follow the steps for sitting on a cushion. You can cross your legs and rest your hands on your knees. You can also keep your feet flat on the floor and rest the back of the left hand on your lap with the palm of your right hand on top of the left hand and thumbs touching. If you need an "energy circuit" for the legs, you can put the bottoms of your feet together on the floor. Experiment.

Breathing Preliminaries – Two Fundamental Breaths

There are two basic breaths that are prominent in the meditation and Yoga world. Most meditators and yogis use one or the other. The basic breath of the Taoists and Yogis begins with controlled deep breathing with the diaphragm. The basic breath of Theravada (pronounced Tair-uh-vah'-dah) Buddhism begins with watching your natural breathing pattern until it deepens on its own from mindfulness. Some people like to argue that THEIR method is the better one, but don't be fooled. Both of these approaches take you to a deeper place. See which one works for you under varying conditions.

Diaphragmatic Breathing

1. *Place your index finger at the bottom of your navel.*

2. Place the middle finger just below it, touching the middle finger and the ring finger below that and the pinky below that. There is no space between your fingers.

3. Press hard into your abdomen with equal pressure from all four fingers.

4. Exhale completely through the nose.

5. Inhale through your nose and allow your abdomen to push out all those fingers.

6. You're doing it correctly if all four fingers are being pushed with equal pressure.

7. Your belly should feel like it's simultaneously pushing forward, into the back, and up and down and therefore "massaging" the internal organs. You should feel it massaging the spine, including the point on the spine behind the navel, and the genital area.

8. Exhale completely through the nose, allowing the diaphragmatic movement to go in reverse. The breath should have roughly the same "force" and sound as the inhale.

It is important that the inhale and exhale be roughly even with the same force. Evenness of breath is both the cause of and result of a healthy nervous system.

If you can keep this breath going throughout the day, you are in for some greatly improved health and vitality. It is the basis of Qigong and some meditation and Yoga techniques.

Variation on Diaphragmatic Breathing – the Yogic Full Breath

1. *Empty the lungs entirely. You can pull your belly in to facilitate the emptying. Relax the belly, letting it pop out into its normal position again.*

2. *Begin a diaphragmatic inhale. Don't fill it all the way.*

3. *In the same inhale, begin filling the middle of your chest (and back), allowing it to expand. Don't fill up all the way.*

4. *Continue the inhale by breathing into your upper chest (and back) and neck. Allow your shoulders to raise a little bit. Now you can fill up.*

5. *Exhale, allowing everything to move in the exact reverse direction as during the inhale.*

6. *Pull your belly in to completely empty the lungs*

7. *Relax your belly, letting it pop out into normal position again.*

8. *Inhale again and so on.*

   The entire inhale is all one continuous flow, as is the exhale. The more you practice, the better it flows. It is one process. The fragments fall away over time.

The Theravada Buddhist breath

1. *However you are breathing, feel it as near as possible to the tip of your nose inside your nostrils where the "cool" sensation of the breath is. You can also focus on the air just under the nostrils where they meet the place above your*

upper lip. Do not follow the breath in and out with your
mind. Just focus on the sensation in your nostrils.

2. *If your mind wanders,* **allow your thoughts to rise and fall**
   like the waves on the ocean. *Silently watch your thoughts*
   when they arise. They are not you. They are just happening.
   That's it. Gently bring your attention back to the air in your
   nostrils.

Your breath will naturally deepen as you concentrate and relax
into the breath. Even if you begin breathing with your chest, your
breath will gradually become more diaphragmatic as you continue
the exercise.

Concentrating on your nostrils during mindfulness meditation
prevents drowsiness. If your problem is drowsiness during
meditation, then this is a good thing to concentrate on. If your
problem is too much thinking, then the navel center (a couple
inches below your navel and a couple inches inward) may be the
place to concentrate. In the Vipassana (Theravada Buddhist
meditation) section, a third point of concentration will be revealed.
All of this information will be repeated more elaborately in that
section.

Detoxification Reactions

Migun Thermatic Jade Massage Beds offers a short video
and a brochure explaining "improvement reactions" from use of
their healing beds. Symptoms may include runny nose, nausea,
swelling, rash, joint pain, dizziness and headaches. These are signs
that the body is detoxifying. Meditation and Yoga sometimes
produce similar "improvement reactions". Know that your body and
mind are purifying and becoming healthier.

When you meditate, you are facing yourself. Impurities bubble up to the surface as the light of consciousness shines on us. Mentally, this can mean sudden irritability, anger or crying. Physically, it can include the "improvement reaction" symptoms mentioned above.

Mental and physical purification are prerequisites for the higher stages of meditation. When experiencing mental "improvement reactions", understand that everyone else is just as screwed up and pathetic as you are. It then becomes easier to face all the "demons" that bubble up.

It also helps not to assume that you are above all that dark stuff. Maybe subconsciously you ARE prejudiced against Chinese people, despite your politically correct upbringing. So what? When it comes up, face it and let it go. We pick up a lot of garbage without realizing it.

Through mental detoxification, your outdated versions of reality, i.e. your outdated symbols that no longer serve, are releasing. You are letting go in order to embrace a deeper, more expansive and more refined perception of reality.

When you are angry at someone, it is harder to see the reality of the situation when confronting them. When you finally relax, it is much easier to see clearly. In the same way, when you let go of long held toxins and harmful emotional patterns, you will see much more clearly in the long run. All your chronic anger, jealousy, etc. is based on beliefs and symbolic structures that are not serving you properly. It is just "frozen" energy. Let it melt.

Drink lots of water during detoxification periods. It will help you release the physical toxins from the cells.

It is best not to worry. Annoying and painful reactions won't be the norm and, when they occur, you will become much freer and healthier. **Let them rise and fall like waves on the ocean**.

Fixing Bad Habits

Do you find yourself worrying about whether other people eat unhealthy foods or smoke cigarettes? Judgment is a very bad habit. It leads to the poisoning of both the mind and the body and inevitably leads to an early death. Judgment is certainly not an act to be performed in front of impressionable children.

Work on fixing your own weaknesses instead of other people's weaknesses and meditation will become easier for you. Meditation may also help you to fix your bad habits.

More Preliminaries for Deeper Meditation

Mindfulness and Relaxing into the Flow

Whether we're breathing, stretching, silently witnessing ourselves, praying to Jesus, practicing Tai Chi Chuan, or whatever, it is important to practice mindfulness and relax into the flow. When performing nondynamic yogic breathing, relax into it until the breath seems to be breathing you. While chanting, relax into the vibrations in the body until the chant begins chanting you. Progressively release tension in the jaw, eyes, spine and the rest of the body. Warm-up exercises prepare the road for this.

Mindfulness simply means paying attention to what you are doing in the moment, whether you're breathing, thinking or making a milkshake. All the exercises in this book will benefit you only if you synchronize them with your full attention.

If this is an abstract concept to you, don't worry. You will learn a few methods for accomplishing these things as you read on. For now, just take a little LSD.

LSD – Love Surrender Devotion

What is love? That's a hard one to answer. Love can be an emotion. However, the truest form of Love is so expansive that it contains all the other emotions. It is the pure spaciousness, stillness and bliss that unites all things.

Consciousness in its purest form is Love and vice versa. When you love something or someone, you get to know it/them much more intimately, right?

When you fall in love, you are totally absorbed. You're certainly concentrating. You can develop this type of absorption in everyday life. Loving absorption brings consciousness and stillness. If you have a memory of falling in love, then you can access this memory whenever you wish to concentrate on something.

The way to Union (Yoga) is through this type of intimacy and knowledge.

When there is a union of love, it is accurate to affirm that the beloved lives in the lover and the lover lives in the beloved. Love causes such similarity and transformation in the lovers that one can say that each one is the other and both of them are one. - St. John of the Cross (Spiritual Songs 12:7)

Now, that's concentration!

You can cultivate love and Love. If you don't have feelings of love in this moment, fake it with the "inner smile" exercise mentioned elsewhere in this book. In a nutshell, you are smiling at yourself and your internal organs, beginning with your third eye, physical eyes and jaw. The more you fake it, the more real and genuine the love becomes, leading eventually to Love. How great is our symbolic imagination!

Always use some form of love cultivation exercise in your warm ups. The inner smile, forgiveness and metta (compassion) practices are ideal for this. They are great tuning mechanisms which point us like a radio dial toward the true Love.

Apply this love to your chanting, breathing, meditation, etc.

Surrender is just what was mentioned a few paragraphs ago. It is relaxing into the flow. "The flow" is not the flow of your desires and subconscious programs which make you whimsical. The flow, once entered, destroys whimsical behavior. You are relaxing into your essence. When thoughts come up, you are not clinging to them nor pushing them away. Everything just is.

As time goes on, the surrendering process becomes more and more refined. There are billions, maybe trillions of little pathways that connect us to the universe. The more conscious this process becomes, the more connections we create with the rest of the universe and therefore ourselves. Think of how many pathways the amoeba has for connecting with the universe. How about a computer? Compare this to a human. Humans are developed to the point where they can consciously increase their connection to the rest of the universe. Some people describe the process as "relaxing into the All".

Surrender takes a little bit of practice to develop as a habit. Cultivating love can help you with this. So can self massage, muscle stretching, chanting, and just about every other exercise in this book.

The following four methods are great for surrendering:

1. Progressively clenching muscles and releasing them during diaphragmatic breathing. You can synchronize this with your breath if that helps: Inhale, hold breath and clench, exhale while gradually releasing.

2. Stretching muscles while "breathing into the stretch". In other words, instead of mentally following the air into the lungs, imagine the breath is entering the muscles that you're stretching instead. Hold the stretch for at

least three diaphragmatic breaths. Some people will say that it requires a seven breath minimum for the brain to register the stretch. Whatever the case, this process brings more consciousness to that set of muscles.

3. The "inner smile"

4. Self massage

All of these exercises are in the warm up portion of this book.

Remember these two words with every exercise you do – **softening and deepening**.

It's funny how you know all this stuff already. In fact, it's hilarious. Sometimes teaching simply involves rearranging information that is already known.

Devotion is commitment and focus. You are devoted to the soul and that which brings wholeness. A Bhakta will say that it is a commitment to loving thoughts of the Beloved and ultimate oneness with the Beloved through Love. Bhaktas have their eyes on the prize. Devotion can be developed through love and surrender. Devotion is the engine that propels you through your spiritual progress. Devotion can also be synonomous with love in many contexts.

The way I learned deep devotion was through chant – singing to the one God in all God's forms and aspects.

Meditation is fruitless without LSD. You hear that, Timothy?

Rising and Falling

Everything rises and falls. Birth, decay, death, rebirth. Buddhists pay special attention to this. Vipassana meditation involves watching this process. The breath rises and falls. Sensations in the body rise and fall. Thoughts rise and fall. Desires rise and fall. Psychic phenomena may, in some cases rise and fall. The Vipassana meditator enters the position of the "silent witness", or the observer, which is the true self. The breath, sensations, desires, thoughts and ecstatic visions are the waves of the ocean. The more you become the silent witness, detached from it all, the closer you are to becoming the ocean.

God (who?) is the deep stillness watching all of the constant flux - the rising and falling. Behind all rising and falling is an infinitely expansive bliss that we can all tap into. This is the transcendent aspect of God. The active principle springs out from this blissful stillness.

Everything that rises and falls is energy. Spirit is that infinite stillness or spaciousness beyond all energy.

Many meditation techniques contain the silent witness element. We can practice being the silent witness in everyday life. Such a skill can be cultivated in meditation and vice versa.

Sensory Orientation

During both warm ups and meditation, it is important to learn how to turn the senses inward. Our eyes should be looking into our body space. Not only does this help with meditation, but it also brings greater humility. We become more focused on healing ourselves and letting that healing spread to others than on trying to save everyone else from themselves. We gradually develop "a mind like a mirror". The sense of oneness between ourselves and others increases, eventually resulting in unconditional love.

Inner Awareness Exercise

You can do this exercise with your eyes open, closed, or a little of both.

1. Relax and take a few diaphragmatic breaths. Relax into the breaths.

2. Clench your jaw, forehead and back of the head. Release and feel the difference.

3. Stretch out your jaw muscles, forehead and back of the head. Breathe into the stretch a few times.

4. Look up at the third eye between your eyebrows. You'll know it when you hit just the right spot. You will feel a gentle strain in the eyes and they will feel still and motionless. Smile at the third eye. Keep breathing diaphragmatically. When your third eye is fully relaxed and filled with love, let that love spread to the jaw. Keep looking into the third eye.

5. When the jaw is relaxed, keep your attention on the third eye. Smile at it some more. Allow the love to flood from the third eye to the rest of the body.

6. If your eyes are not shut by now, shut them for awhile. "See" your whole body with your third eye. If you don't, then just imagine it. Over time, it will become more real.

7. Open your eyes while still watching yourself with your third eye. Notice how it feels the same as when your eyes were closed. Notice how it feels different.

8. Close your eyes again and feel your whole body with your third eye with the love – which is consciousness - still trickling down. Relax into the sensations in the body. Open your eyes and repeat, noticing any differences and similarities.

Sensory Orientation Exercise: Practicing Presence with Others

This exercise becomes easier as you become more in tune with the feelings in your body. The exercises in the muscles and soft tissues section are very important, partially for this reason.

1. *Tuck in your chin a little bit toward your throat and imagine a string pulling your head up from the baby soft spot at the top of the head. "Stack" your vertebrae one on top of another from the bottom up.*

2. *Stare straight ahead, neither squinting nor widening the eyes. Do not stare intently.*

3. *Smile at your third eye between the eyebrows. Smile at your jaw.*

4. *Pay attention to your relaxed jaw, your relaxed eyes, your relaxed hands, your center of gravity (2 inches below your navel and 2 inches in). Relax into your center of gravity. You can use the "tense and release" or "clench and release" methods to relax these parts.*

5. *Defocus the eyes. Soften the gaze and the eyes, looking outward and inward at the same time. "Feel" inside the body while looking at nothing in particular. Be conscious of the whole field of consciousness.*

6. *Be conscious of everything without attraction and repulsion – i.e. clinging to comfort and pushing away discomfort. Be present with yourself and the environment.*

7. *Be mindful of the Earth beneath your feet and the sky above you.*

8. *Now, if there is a person or crowd available, be present with that person, feeling them within your own body. Relax and be present with all the feelings in your body. Don't let any part of the experience obstruct the smooth flow of breath. **Soften** into your breath **and deepen your experience.** Obstructed breath means obstructed consciousness.*

At first, you may feel only your reactions to the person. Over time, you may be able to feel more of their energy. Over more time, your distinctions between the internal world and the external world will gradually fall away. They are not separate. Our symbolic thinking makes them separate. It was a convenient mechanism at one point. Let it go eventually if you haven't already.

Welcome to the present moment. You are moving beyond seeing a person from conditioned consciousness and you're on your way to beginning to see them as they are, beyond the symbols you created... AND you're cultivating inner awareness – the awareness that melts all your unneeded symbols and the chronic emotions that are based on these symbols.

All the warm up exercises in your routine should help you turn your sensory orientation inward. When you chant, you can close your eyes and relax into it, lovingly **softening and deepening** into your body, into yourself, into the chant, as time goes on. The more you **soften and deepen**, the more inward the sensory orientation becomes. Breathing into a stretch also brings your attention inward.

After a dynamic exercise, close your eyes and take three breaths in the prayer position (hands folded in front of the heart like a statue of Mary). **Soften** into each breath **and deepen** your self awareness.

By the time you begin your meditation practice, your senses should be inwardly oriented.

Going Deeper Yet

Your Magic Portal(s)

Everyone has a unique way of entering that special state of mind. Do you have a favorite song, especially one that speaks to your soul? Do you have a favorite nature spot? A favorite writing that touches your soul? Scriptural passages? Poetry? A favorite dancing style? A chant? A vivid, uplifting memory? A victorious memory? A memory of a very serene state of mind? An entrancing musical instrument? Do you remember what it feels like? What it smells like? What it looks like? Do you like to go on nature walks, including "urban" ones? How do you feel after walking and absorbing nature into yourself?

Think back. You may have some powerful tools to warm up for meditation with. Add them to your routine and your daily life.

Levels of Personhood

We all hear the words "mind, body and spirit". Some people may describe Yoga as the act of unifying mind, body and spirit. A solid routine should incorporate these three levels of personhood somehow. Warm ups "tune" the mind, body and energy. Meditation is accessing Spirit (stillness, spaciousness). Stillness automatically integrates form and energy, aligning them with itself.

More specifically, a good complete warm up should include the **"7+1 Tuning Method"**:

1. *Muscles and Soft Tissues (stretching, limbering joints, shaking, massage, Yoga postures)*

2. *Energy and Chakras (energy work, soft flowing movement, gathering chi, cultivating chi and physical energy)*

3. *Nature (communing with a real or imagined nature spot, Chi Kung nature exercises)*

4. *Emotions (chant, forgiveness work, gratitude, lovingkindness visualizations, loving memories, inner smile)*

5. *Intellect (reading inspiring words or scripture, thinking about spiritual concepts)*

6. *Imagination (visualization, which includes feeling, hearing, etc.)*

7. *Breath (pranayama or yogic breathing, diaphragmatic breathing, other breathing exercises)*

8. *Spirit (meditation)*

    You don't have time for all this? Just pick a few exercises that work best or use your intuition. For tips on the order of the exercises, read on.

The Four Styles of Information Processing

Neurolinguistic Programming is a style of therapy which resulted from detailed research into which therapeutic styles were most effective. One of their biggest gems is their emphasis on "learning styles".

The four learning styles are:

1. Visual

2. Auditory

3. Kinesthetic

4. Auditory Digital

Visual processers tend to think and receive information in pictures. They are likely to acknowledge a point by saying "I see what you're saying" and may find it helpful to learn something by watching or through an instruction manual.

Audio people think and receive in sounds and verbal information. They are likely to learn by listening.

Kinesthetic people tend to get the feel for things. They are likely to learn by doing.

Auditory Digital people tend to try to "make sense" of the information received, often through internal dialogue. This one is often lumped in with auditory learning.

There are tests on the internet for finding out which learning style is your strongest one if you haven't figured out where you fit already.

Some techniques can be adapted for different learning styles. If you're doing a visualization and you're a kinesthetic processor, then emphasize the feeling element in the visualization (don't ignore the sounds and sights, however). Chakra meditations can be versatile, too. You can "feel energy" rather than "see light".

Choose some warm-ups that fit into your learning style. However If you're visual, don't neglect the muscles just because you're visual.

Vipassana meditation is Kinesthetic as is my main meditation technique – the Kriya Yoga of Yogananda and Babaji. I am mainly kinesthetic and would not trade Kriya for anything.

Warm Ups "Tune" the Mind and Body for Meditation

A holistic warm up workout should have a profound effect on your meditation, especially if you have been following all the principles of intertwine, momentum, sensory orientation and consistency.

Some immediate goals for a workout include a slower heart rate (by the end, but not necessarily during the dynamic exercises), a sense of "connection" to the body (grounding), deeper breath, calm and clear nerve energy, slower brainwaves and an inward sensory orientation.

Also pay attention to the possibility of seeing light in the forehead, when your eyes are closed, as well as inner sounds, pulsations and frequencies. In advanced students, a perception of inner light and sound in the forehead or other areas of the body become more pronounced. Such students may benefit from light and sound meditations followed by techniques which allow one to gradually transcend light and sound.

If nothing else, you should aim at experiencing a feeling of "opening". You will feel like you're suddenly breaking out of the trance created by the mental programs that run throughout the day. Things that may have bothered you earlier begin to subside or become clearer.

Deep meditation requires "tuning your mental radio" as swami Satchitananda says. Not only that, but it requires tuning your entire being toward an inward state of mind and, eventually, to an inwardoutwardspringingoutfromtheinward state of mind or something like that.

The Five Minute Intertwine Revisited

You think you read this one enough times? Now, stop reading. Take a few deep breaths. Stretch. That's it. Look up at your third eye and sing Om Shanti Shanti Shanti (Om Divine Peace Divine Peace Divine Peace). Massage your scalp. No one's looking. I won't tell your friends that you massage your scalp. Scratch it hard and briskly if you have to. Now, Hokey Pokey. Sing it Loud!

Developing a Routine

Movement into Stillness, Form into Spirit

Developing a regular routine that works for you may require a little bit of trial and error. Here are some tips for developing a routine.

Some of the warm up exercises in this book are "hot" exercises. This means that they involve either vigorous body movement or breath and they generate heat in the body. The contraindications for such exercises are included in the introduction to this book. Relatively good health is recommended for such exercises.

It is my common practice to begin a routine with hot exercises and work my way into the "cooler" exercises – the ones that are soft, flowing or motionless – and then stationary ones whether it's morning or evening. However, some like to do this only in the evening and the reverse in the morning. If you need more energizing in the morning and less meditation, then try this method. Experiment a little bit.

Let's assume it is evening. Begin with hot muscle exercises, shaking, slapping and limbering. Try some hot breathing exercises such as the Breath of Fire. After that, maybe some energy or slow movement exercises. Slip in some self massage and inner smiles here and there throughout the routine. Add a couple things from your magic portals list, including a calming chant. Next, try lovingkindness work. Then, do your more balancing pranayamas and breathing afterward. You're moving toward stillness at this point. Lovingkindness visualizations can also follow this. Now, you're ready to meditate.

One thing that should be noted is that many Yoga teachers insist that the nondynamic pranayama breathing exercises must be performed after stretching and movement for the effects to be optimized.

Don't get overwhelmed. This is the long version. You can pick out just three or four things and then meditate for five minutes. It's ok.

Remember the following:

Dynamic → Slow and Meditative → Mental and Emotional (less movement)→ Breath → Stillness

And more specifically:

Gross form → Gross and Subtle Form → Subtle Form → Breath of Life → Spirit

Sometimes, during the warm ups, you may end up slipping into a meditative state. You have limbered up your "energy and form" aspects and have entered the "spirit" phase. Flow with it.

You may even encounter spontaneous movement and spontaneous breath exercises. They may resemble Chi Gong, Tai Chi, Yoga stretching, slapping, humming, sounds, singing, etc . Some say that this is only a cleansing process, i.e. the clearing of blockages. However, there is more.

You have engaged in activities that carried you from form (including energy) into stillness (spirit). From spirit, effortless action results, and such action is always the correct action in the moment. You have united the transcendent nature of spirit with the active nature.

The formula: Form → Spirit → Form

The first Form came from an intellectual idea of what to do to find stillness. When you find stillness, you access Spirit. From Spirit, you re-enter Form beyond symbolic intellectual concepts, from a place of transcendence.

This is the "Real Yoga". It will greatly help you to follow your inner guidance in daily life. Remember what it feels like.

Intuitive living begins with receiving intuitive "hunches" and acting on them. Just like Karma Yoga, the process becomes more refined until you are just following the movement of spirit into form.

In this case, intuition and action become one motion rather than two distinct parts. An "inner marriage" has been realized. The two have become one. There's no intuitive feeling or concept to listen to. You are just doing it. If you wish to give it a name, call it "intuaction" if you wish. Don't confuse it with the life coaching term, however.

Let's look at Shiva. Shiva is the transcendent reality. Out of this transcendent stillness comes Shiva again, in the form of Nataraja, Lord of the Dance. You can also use the imagery of Shiva and Shakti making love if you wish. Sing to Shiva for a while to verify this. You just may become Shiva, who will show you the meaning of this concept.

God always leads us toward this "cleansing process". The process integrates us where there is a block in the flow – where we are not whole. When we are doing exactly what Spirit instructs, we are "cleansing" aka "burning". We, as vessels, become clearer as the Divine expresses itself more fully through us. We are learning to step out of the way and to "let go let God". Such a learning process does not happen through living passively, but by acting according to our deepest intuition.

Anyway, your entire routine should look something like this:

Dynamic Exercises (gross form) → Calming Movement Exercises (form) → Inner Exercises (subtle form) → Meditation (Spirit) → Projection of Energy (Prayers, Supplication, Healing Work, Manifesting, Action) (Form) → "Bathing"- Basking in the Peace → Integration of Spirit into the Sensory World (Union)

Remember that all form dissolves into Spirit, just as waves dissolve into the ocean, sound dissolves into silence and light dissolves into space. We're gradually moving toward stillness.

Again, If time is an issue, just pick and choose a short combination of exercises that works best for you, then meditate for five minutes or as long as you can. Choose few enough exercises so that you don't have to rush or immediately run for the door when you're finished. Skip Projection and shorten Bathing. Don't skip Integration.

Projection? Bathing? Is he speaking Greek? These are explained in the next three sections. See? Now you have to come back to this section later. Ha Ha Ha.

After you've studied a few of the exercises and begin developing a routine, come back and read this section again.

So far, you've learned a structured approach for your warm up and meditation routine. At some point, you may develop a more intuitive approach. You may just stop in the middle of muscle exercises and slip into deep meditation or spontaneous exercises followed by meditation. Your intuition will increasingly guide you as time goes on. In any type of training, we always start with structure and move into more intuitively guided approaches. Have you ever spent a few years practicing a musical instrument? It's a similar process.

There is always an optimum Magic Portal in each moment. You may be performing a formal practice routine that takes you to a wonderful place most of the time, but today it's just not happening. Perhaps you need to break the routine and find out what really takes you to that special place in this moment. Maybe you just need to be singing or playing your banjo before meditation today.

Projection of Energy – Prayer, Healing, Manifesting, Action

Gary Clyman, Chi Kung master and developer of the Personal Power Training program, insists that real Chi Kung consists of the following process:

1. *Gathering chi*

2. *Cultivating chi*

3. *Circulating chi in the body through the Microcosmic Orbit*

4. *Projecting Chi*

There are many schools of Chi Kung, and many will disagree with Gary. However, a lot of Chi Kung programs do have a method of "projecting energy". Projection usually takes on the form of hands on healing or manifesting your desired life in the form of will development, visualization and destroying negative programming.

There is medical Chi Kung, magical Chi Kung, Shamani[...]
probably more. Gary practices magical Chi Kung, or "[...]
the Universe" as he calls it, combined with the development of the
will.

Some meditation teachers will say that one must not
engage in manifestation work after meditation because it may
interfere with the integration and bathing stages in some people.
However, it may be the best time to do such things. It is the
moment when prayer is most effective. Only you know what works
for you.

There are many books on effective prayer, visualization,
manifestation and the Law of Attraction. This book is not one of
them. However, recommendations may come in handy:

1. *The Secret*

2. *The Abraham-Hicks Collection*

3. *Creative Visualization by Shakti Gawain*

4. *ThetaHealing™ by Vianna Stibal (order at
   www.thetahealing.com)*

5. *The Isaiah Effect by Greg Braden*

6. *Any book or program by Jose Silva (The Silva Method)*

Both ThetaHealing and The Isaiah Effect reveal the science
of effective prayer. Theta Healing combines all the elements of
manifestation work with a Theta brainwave state (between 4 and 8
cycles per second), the state of waking dreams in which you watch
the Creator answer your prayers instantly. One method for entering
a Theta state is included in a chakra exercise in this book. An even

better approach is to enter an Alpha, Alpha/Theta or Theta state by following the steps in this book and then use the Theta method in the chakra clearing exercise before visualization.

Medical Chi Kung is similar to some of the methods of Therapeutic Touch, a form of Laying on of Hands, but it is more developed and based on thousands of years of experience. It begins with self healing and meditation and externalizes into the world in the form of healing others of physical and mental imbalances.

Projecting does not necessarily mean formalized manifestation work or formalized healing work. All meditation practices should have a projecting component whether it is part of your routine or not. When your "cup runneth over", the rest of the world should benefit somehow. The more you access Spirit, the more you will listen to the outward movement that comes from it. Your intuition is your guide on this.

During a routine, projecting could just mean "Real Yoga", spontaneous movement which springs out from the stillness. This brings practice for the real projection, which is active engagement in the world (Karma Yoga) – a step toward Heaven on Earth. Manifesting, in its purest form, also brings practice in bringing Heaven to Earth. Formalized healing brings practice of the engagement in our purpose in life - healing ourselves and others. All these things are intertwined and teach us that all appropriate action in the world comes from the stillness within.

Supplicating prayers and visualization are useless without listening to intuitions which both precede them and follow them. We must be clear about what we pray for and align it with our higher purpose.

We must also be ready to follow our "hunches" or guidance which follow prayer and remove whatever weaknesses or blocks that are in the way.

Consider the following story:

A Rabbi was shipwrecked on an uncharted desert island. He prayed and prayed and prayed for God to save him. He conducted the prayer perfectly by commanding that God save him, thanking God for already granting the prayer and actually imagining the prayer being granted with all the good feelings that go along with that. At last, he was certain that God would save him.

Along came a man in a sailboat. "Dude, you need a ride?"

"No," said the Rabbi. "God will save me."

"Good luck!"

Along came a woman in a Yacht wearing medallions, shades and fur. "You look like you could use a lift."

"God will save me," said the Rabbi. The woman sailed away, sipping on a Pina colada.

Along came George Burns himself, puffing on a cigar in his fishing boat.

The Rabbi thought for a minute: He kind of looks like God. Nah! God would be wearing a yarmulke.

"Can I help you with anything?" asked George.

"No thanks. God will save me."

After George left, the Rabbi was beginning to feel uneasy. He jumped up and down, angry that God hadn't saved him yet.

Deep, thunderous laughter descended from Heaven. The Rabbi was fuming.

"Why are you laughing?! I'm stuck out here and you haven't saved me!"

A puff of cigar smoke blew out of Heaven, filling the sky. God put his straight face back on and said, "C'mon, dude! I sent three boats for you!" before laughing so hard he fell out of the sky, plunging into the sea.

Remaining "inward" and saying "it will all work out" will not save us. When you pray, be ready to be put to work, no matter what weaknesses and insecurities stand between you and the accomplished task. Complete the projection process by following your hunches while remaining inward at the same time. That is, at least until you achieve "intuaction".

In other words, when you "impregnate the universe", allow it to impregnate you in turn. The Rabbi thought he was separate from the universe when, in fact, he was the center of the universe. Let the universe do its work through you.

Remain detached, letting the hunches come. Don't hold Spirit up at gunpoint demanding intuitions.

Just think. If all of us let go of our fears and truly did these things, the whole "machine" we complain about every day would just fall apart. Destroy the system!!!!!!!!!!!!!!! Meditation is very punk.

Realize that your job is not to save the world. Some people burn out and become selfish and cynical after trying to save humanity. Align yourself with the dictates of Spirit and do that.

This whole intuition into action process is also part of the "Integrating" process mentioned below. There is a lot of overlap between all the stages.

"Bathing" – Basking in the Peace

You've concluded your formal meditation and now you are bathing in the resulting peace. Hatha Yogis do this in the "corpse pose" (lying on the back) after pranayama. That's all there is to it. Bask in the peace.

It is best not to immediately "get up and go" after meditation. It is better if that happens in stages. Bathing is one of these stages.

Integration – Integrating Meditation into the Sensory World

Your formal meditation practice made you inward oriented. Now, it's time to integrate the internal and the external world.

After bathing, open and close your eyes a few times. Next, you can try the last exercise in the Sensory Orientation section or the standing posture exercise in the Posture section. Then, affirm that you will listen to your intuition throughout the day (or evening). Look around and connect with your environment. Afterward, integrate your higher consciousness into every activity.

When your sensory orientation is looking inward and outward at the same time, such as in the standing posture exercise, then you know you are on the right track.

If it is night time, you can go back into bathing after integration if you wish. It will be more integrated.

Authentic Connection Breath or "Integrating Breath":

Try the following exercise to integrate your internal consciousness with the external world.

1. *Breathe in with a diaphragmatic breath. Breath is consciousness. Be conscious of yourself and honor yourself with a smile.*

2. *Exhale with the same force and volume as the inhale. Be conscious of the external environment and honor everything in it with a smile.*

3. *You can begin by honoring your immediate environment on the exhale and gradually expand to the whole neighborhood, nation, Earth, Planet Vulcan, etc. after many exhales.*

4. *Repeat as long as you wish.*

This section explains the initial stage of integration after formal practice. See the Grounding Meditation into Everyday Life section for tips on the later integration stages.

A Word about the Imagination

"Symbolitus"

In my first symbolic logic class, we studied argument structures such as:

If p then q

p

Therefore q

This can also be represented as:

$p \rightarrow q$

p

$\vdash q$

For those who don't know already, the p's and q's can represent any statement that is either true or false, such as "my name is bob", "it is raining", etc. The symbolic structure can represent the following statement:

If he asks me out, then I will faint. He is asking me out. Therefore, I will faint.

Some of the folks in class minded their p's and q's too much and got lost in the symbols. The professor would get very frustrated and say "C'mon! We're speaking English! Don't you people speak English?!"

It is too easy to drown in the symbols and forget the reality behind the symbols. The reality behind the symbols, in this case, was actual English sentences that we normally understand with no problem. The professor called this condition "Symbolitus".

Let's say you decide to start a commune in the countryside. You have an image of what that looks like. Everyone can do whatever they wish without The Man bringing them down. It should be open to all, etc.

You study other communes and decide that some of them are pretty "stuck up". They screen people before they let them in. That's not a free society.

You roll out the red carpet for participants of your new utopia. After a couple of weeks, you discover that almost everyone who shows up has a drinking problem. However, You don't want to tell them what to do in a miniature free society.

A couple of months pass and you realize that no one's pulling their own weight. A lot of fighting is going on.

Years pass and people come and go, most of them drunk. Residents find travelling drinking buddies in town and invite them to live on the farm. Everyone who does not share the urge to drink every day tends to stay clear away from the place.

If you keep holding onto the intellectual concept of your ideal society, the whole operation will fall apart. That is one manifestation of Symbolitus.

Our whole life journey is a refining process between theory and reality. Here's another example:

A nation decides to go "communist", or at least a few people with a lot of followers who have the means to create this reality make this decision. "The People" finally get everything they need to live their daily lives without worry. The other people are not part of this symbolic group called "The People".

"The People" are fully aligned with the views and symbolic models of reality of the new powerholders. They certainly receive the goodies in life. They have "freedom" to do anything they want. It is certainly a free country these days.

The other people are not so aligned with the new order. They end up poor or in jail. "The People" cannot understand why these people can be so opposed to a good thing. All they have to do is act more like "The People" and they will be fed. They must just be aligned with the evil order of the past and therefore the embodiment of pure evil.

"The People" become the embodiment of pure evil in the eyes of the other people.

Capitalism does the same thing. Economists create academically sound symbolic structures that usually favor the powerful. The theories clearly demonstrate that what is good for the powerful is also good for everyone else.

Before long you get urban uprisings, 911's and most of the third world nations spitting on the symbols of the more powerful nation. In the minds of the people on the powerful side of the fence, there's no problem. We're helping these ungrateful brats. They must be pure evil. Power always denies that power exists.

The Romans experienced terrorists. The British Empire was a model of "peace" in the world. All their academic theories "proved" it. Gandhi appeared to the puzzlement of good Englishmen. The founding fathers of the United States were even more puzzling. The situation just did not "compute" within the prevailing British theory.

And on and on it goes... Symbolitus.

Tyrants don't know that they're tyrants because they are stuck in theory which, in turn, is stuck within an ego structure. They may even believe they're saving the world. Unfortunately, their subjects are also stuck in theory.

Symbolitus is the condition of being so caught up in symbolic models of reality that we're blinded to reality.

Symbolitus is universal. Even our perception of a tree in front of us is symbolic. Does an amoeba experience a tree in the same way we do? Are we really at the summit of reality as human beings? Our perception is wrong and so is the amoeba's. Our connection to the universe just happens to be a little more complex.

The entire ego structure is composed of symbols. This includes national and tribal ego structures and those of empires. We mistake these symbol structures for the reality of who we really are.

Meditation is the process of gradually seeing things as they really are.

Are you experiencing Déjà vu? Some things cannot be repeated enough.

The Role of the Imagination in Meditation, Intuitive Development and the Law of Attraction

Beginning remote viewers typically launch their practice by visualizing a room or some place that has verifiable contents, usually from outside the room. The viewer will note every detail in their imaginary model of the selected location before physically checking the room to find out where they were correct and incorrect.

Eventually, the viewer's observations become more and more accurate until they can mentally enter any building and see the contents within. The symbolic imagination was the initial tuning tool which carried the viewer to the reality beyond the tool.

There is one yogic breath called the "short breath". You imagine the breath to begin in the Petuitary gland in the center of the brain and end at the fontanel, the baby soft spot at the top of the head. You follow the breath up with your mind on the inhale, but not on the exhale. It is a love offering to God in the crown – soul consciousness merging with God consciousness.

At first, you need to use your imagination to follow this energy channel. Your imagination provides an approximation of what's really happening. Over time, the approximation becomes more and more real until you are just feeling energy moving along that actual channel.

In some healing arts, a practitioner accesses the presence of Spirit, forms a prayer and then witnesses the healing occurring in the "client". The witnessing occurs in symbolic form. For example, the practitioner may witness light or a feeling of blissful love entering the person's body, a group of plumbers working on the digestive system or some other symbolic representation of actual healing occurring. It all depends on how the practitioner's brain wishes to interpret the very real changes that are happening. There are no plumbers there. However, behind the plumber symbol is a very real process.

All of our sensory processing is symbolic. It's all an interpretation by our brains. Again, an amoeba will see a different tree than we do. The amoeba connects to the universe through different channels than we do, so the interpretation is much different.

Just as the monkey mind transforms into Hanuman (pure devotion), becoming our ally, so our symbolic structures of reality can become powerful friends rather than the troublemakers they often are.

Every accomplished goal begins in the imagination. The imagination is a tuning tool. Strengthen your imagination and you will accomplish a lot more.

Remember this in your meditations.

The "7+1 Tuning Method" - Some Warm up Exercises

Do you remember the "7+1" tunings?

They are:

1. *Muscles and Soft Tissues (stretching, limbering joints, shaking, massage, Yoga postures)*

2. *Energy and Chakras (energy work, soft flowing movements, chi gathering and cultivation)*

3. *Nature (communing with a real or imagined nature spot, Chi Kung nature exercises)*

4. *Emotions (chant, forgiveness work, lovingkindness visualizations, loving memories, inner smile)*

5. *Intellect (reading inspiring words or scripture, pondering spiritual concepts)*

6. *Imagination (visualization, which includes feeling, hearing, smelling, etc.)*

7. *Breath (pranayama or yogic breathing, diaphragmatic breathing, other breathing exercises)*

8. *Spirit (meditation)*

Here's a tip for proceeding. Experiment for a while. Get a good feel for what works for you. Stick with a good routine. Some of the exercises offer their greatest treasures after much daily practice, especially the inner power and energy cultivation exercises.

Some of the exercises in the warm up section are actually great meditation practices in themselves. If you slip into a deep meditative state during one of them, perhaps you found your compatible method. In such cases, slip into meditation with detachment, following the flow of breath, etc, and just allow things to **rise and fall like waves on the ocean**. Don't get excited. Just experience.

"The Inner Smile" – Qigong's Most Obvious Secret

The inner smile is a technique that is taught by Mantak Chia, a Qigong master and author as well as Ken Cohen, another Qigong master and author, and by Thich Nhat Hanh, a Mahayana Buddhist author.

When you smile at another person, you are filling them with chi and allowing them to relax. Defenses drop. Their day becomes brighter.

We can do the same thing to ourselves. Our minds and internal organs will thank us for it by functioning more efficiently with greater health. If you just wish to relax your muscles, the inner smile is one method you can use.

If you have diabetes, then the focusing on the adrenal glands at the top of each kidney might prove beneficial. It will at least stimulate the pancreas. You don't have to pinpoint where they are exactly. You only have to have the intent to smile at your adrenals and the approximate location to do so. You may eventually pinpoint them in time as the awareness grows with regular practice.

You can perform the smile exercise any way you wish. If you wish for a formalized approach, then read the following instructions.

Instructions for the Inner Smile

1. *Smile at the third eye between the eyebrows and a little bit inside the forehead. Allow the forehead to relax.*

2. *Smile at your two physical eyes and allow them to relax.*

3. *Smile at your jaw and allow it to relax.*

4. *Proceed with the neck, shoulders, arms, hands, internal organs in the upper torso, internal organs in the lower torso, all the way down. Be as elaborate as you wish.*

5. *Mantak Chia recommends concluding this exercise by circling back up toward the Tan Tien, your center of gravity, which is 2 inches below the navel and an inch or two inward, and ending there. The navel Tan Tien is the best place to store energy. Some practices end their circuits in the upper chakras which can lead to overheating of the brain. The brain is not good at storing chi. See "Gathering Chi into your Navel Tan Tien" in the Muscles and Soft Tissues Section to learn a good method to return chi to its origin (the navel).*

Clench and Release – A Gem from Hatha Yoga

The learning of relaxation often comes from deliberate tension. Therefore, use tension to loosen tension.

Clench and Release

1. *Tighten the muscles in your left foot and ankle. Release. Breathe diaphragmatically into the foot and feel the difference. Repeat if necessary. Repeat this step for the right foot.*

2. *Repeat for the left and right calf. Then the thighs, butt and genitals, lower abdomen, upper abdomen, arms, shoulders and hands, neck, jaw, entire head.*

All this should take a few minutes the first time. It becomes quicker over time.

Stretch and Release

This exercise combines muscles and breath. Breath is awareness, which brings relaxation. If you ever feel the urge to do this exercise spontaneously, do so.

Stretch and Release

1. *Breathe diaphragmatically and pay attention to where you are tense in the body.*
2. *Stretch wherever it feels right to do so.*
3. *Breathe into that stretch three to seven times (experiment with both numbers of breaths to determine which works for you).*
4. *Release the stretch and feel the difference.*

Note: If you stretch one arm then, after release, pay attention to both arms while noticing the differences in how both of them feel. Then, stretch the other arm.

Now you have three methods for relaxing any or all parts of the body. You can use these methods with any other exercise to enhance the benefits. Check yourself periodically for tension in the body.

The fourth method of relaxation is self massage. One method of self massage is in the Muscles and Soft Tissues section.

Exercises for the Muscles and Soft Tissues

Warm ups for the muscles have the effect of grounding and clearing. They disperse stagnant energy and bring us out of the clouds and into our bodies. The sexual/physical energy, known in Chinese as "jing", becomes more balanced as do our "lower chakras" – the perineum and tailbone energy center, the sexual energy center behind the pubic bone in the spine, the navel energy center (or "Navel Tan Tien") and the solar plexus.

Anything that instills feeling and awareness in the body is a grounding exercise. Grounding is a very important part of any meditation program, especially for people who are spacey, overly discursive, anxious or get easily overwhelmed.

Incorporating muscle exercises and self massage brings a suppleness to the body and therefore to the mind. The more supple we are, the more versatile we become as vessels of Spirit.

Without proper conditioning of the whole body in spiritual work, the circuitry may get overloaded, resulting in pain in the third eye, itching, numbness, tingling, excessive muscle spasms, a feeling of going crazy, general damage of the higher centers among other symptoms. Neglect of the "lower centers" can sometimes result in these unwanted symptoms if kundalini energy is prematurely aroused in the lower spine. People are sometimes misdiagnosed with schizophrenia and other disorders as a result of such ungrounded awakening of the circuitry.

Neglect or repression of jing can also lead to "fire and brimstone" mentalities, objectification of women (in men) as distracters of men, fundamentalist thinking and other unhealthy mindsets that are the polar opposite to the overindulgence of the senses. This is another false dichotomy that can plague monasteries, religious orders and entire societies. All these sexual perversions can be summed up in one word: Patriarchy.

Therefore, don't be "above" your lower centers or anything else. Your genitals are not "down there". They are not separate from you. If you are above physical and sexual energy, then you will also place yourself above and separate from other people, leading to thoughts of superiority.

Often, in the meditation world, we try to appear "holy" and set an example. It's all hogwash. Pure poppycock! It comes from a desire to exhibit a pre-determined "image" to others. This can only hinder you in your quest to surrender to the flow which comes from the inner stillness. That's no example to anyone. Let go of such crazy images, or at least work in that direction.

Stretching and Compressing the Spine

You can do this one in any position, including standing. As your spine loosens, you may feel inclined to do some other stretches or head and shoulder rolls. Go with the flow.

1. *Without moving your limbs, stretch your spine vertically as much as possible, making yourself as tall as possible. Do this one vertebra at a time. Keep arms at sides the whole time.*
2. *Shrink your spine, making yourself as short as possible (don't move your legs). Feel each vertebra. Feel the vertebrae stacking together, condensing.*
3. *Repeat this a few times.*
4. *Place your hands in prayer position, just like Mother Mary – palms together in front of the chest. Take three diaphragmatic breaths, **softening** into each breath **and***

deepening your experience while feeling the new sensations in the body. Process these feelings fully.

Shake up

1. *Stand with feet about a shoulder width apart.*
2. *Lift your left foot and shake it. Let your breath run wild.*
3. *Lift your right foot and shake it.*
4. *Shake your hips side to side.*
5. *Shake your torso.*
6. *Shake your arms.*
7. *Inhale diaphragmatically through the nose. Exhale through your mouth, making a continuous 'h' sound, while shaking your head from side to side. Let the sound from your mouth wobble with you. Make sure that your cheeks are wobbling. Shake out any distracting thoughts from your head.*
8. *Repeat step 7 at least four times.*
9. *Place your hands in prayer position, just like Mother Mary – palms together in front of the chest. Take three diaphragmatic breaths, **softening** into each breath **and deepening** your experience while feeling the new sensations in the body. Process these feelings fully.*

Twist up

Twist up is for limbering the joints and spine.

1. *Stand with feet about a shoulder width apart.*
2. *Place all your weight on the center of your right foot. Bend your right knee, but keep your balance.*
3. *Place your left foot a little bit behind you. Only the big toe is touching the ground. Place no weight on the big toe.*

4. *Rotate your left foot in a big circle three times without moving your big toe. First counterclockwise. Repeat clockwise.*

5. *Switch feet and repeat the whole process.*

6. *Place your feet and knees together (very important for injury prevention). Grab your knees with your hands. Make circles with your knees – counterclockwise three times, then clockwise three times. Put your hips into it.*

7. *Place feet a shoulder width apart again.*

8. *Grab your hips with your hands. Rotate your hips in big circles counterclockwise three times, then clockwise three times. Make a wide enough circle so that you feel it afterward.*

9. *Keep your hands on your hips. Without moving your hips, rotate your whole torso counterclockwise three times, then clockwise three times. While you're doing this, make sure that your shoulders and head are following your movements. If you're facing forward, in the "North" of the circle, your shoulders and upper back should point forward. When you arrive at "East", let your shoulders point to the right. You should really feel this in the lower back.*

10. *Do the backstroke a few times with your arms. Then reverse the direction of your arms like you're an Olympic swimmer. Afterward, you can rotate your hands by the wrist if you like.*

11. *Roll your shoulders backwards a few times, then forward a few times.*

12. *Roll your head counterclockwise a few times (from a helicopter's point of view), then clockwise a few times.*

13. *Place your hands in prayer position, just like Mother Mary – palms together in front of the chest. Take three*

*diaphragmatic breaths, **softening** into each breath **and deepening** your experience while feeling the new sensations in the body. Process these feelings fully.*

If you need to spend extra time on any of these parts, do so. This exercise limbers up the spine. Limbering the spine enhances everything else.

Wait a minute. Your eyes did not get a workout.

Eye Exercise

1. *Look up. Widen the eyes a little bit. Notice you can see the shadow of your eye sockets and maybe part of your nose. Don't strain too much. Just a little bit.*
2. *Rotate your eyes to the left in a counterclockwise circle. Go slowly enough so that you are always looking at the eye sockets wherever you are at in the circle. Be fully attentive of the eye sockets.*
3. *Make three circles with your eyes. Then reverse direction and do three more circles.*
4. *You may be tempted to breathe erratically during this exercise. Keep the breath smooth and diaphragmatic.*
5. *When finished, relax into the eye between the eyebrows while enjoying the sensations in the eyes.*
6. *Rub your hands together briskly, generating a lot of heat in your palms. Place your palms over your eyes and absorb the energy, magnetism and heat.*
7. *Massage your eyes around the sockets in a circular manner. Shake your hands and fingers briskly like you're shaking off stagnant energy.*
8. *Place your hands in prayer position, just like Mother Mary – palms together in front of the chest. Take three*

diaphragmatic breaths, **softening** into each breath **and deepening** your experience while feeling the new sensations in the body. Process these feelings fully.

Toe Touching, Spinal Bounce

This is another good one for loosening the hips and the spine.

1. *Stand with your feet a shoulder width apart.*
2. *Bend down and touch your toes. Don't bend the knees. You should feel the stretch in the backs of your legs.*
3. *Breathe into the stretch seven times.*
4. *Bounce up and down a little bit with arms dangling.*
5. *Keep your body and head where they are. Fold your arms like you're Bruno the doorman at the night club. Your hands are folded under your head. Gravity is pulling your arms down.*
6. *Bounce up and down, shaking your spine loose. Do this for awhile.*
7. *Starting with your tailbone, lift your body up, slowly stacking one vertebra on top of the other as you lift your body. Stop when you've stacked the highest vertebra in your neck onto the second highest.*
8. *Place your hands in prayer position, just like Mother Mary – palms together in front of the chest. Take three diaphragmatic breaths, **softening** into each breath **and deepening** your experience while feeling the new sensations in the body. Process these feelings fully.*

Spinal Twist

Further limbering of the spine. You may do this in sitting or standing posture.

1. *Put your hands on their corresponding shoulders. Thumbs are on the back of the shoulders. Elbows are pointing perfectly to the right and left respectively and parallel with the floor.*
2. *Inhale and twist your upper body to the left. Your nose is following your torso, pointing straight ahead in relation to the torso.*
3. *Exhale and twist to the right as far as possible.*

Yoga Stretch

Here's one from Hatha Yoga.

1. *Lie down on the floor on your back. Take a long inhale through the nose and hold.*
2. *Lift your legs. Tuck your chin into your chest and lift up your head and chest. Only your butt is touching the floor. Your hands are resting on top of your thighs.*
3. *Exhale through the nose while pulling your toes back toward you, pointing your toes as much as you can toward your head. You'll feel the stretch in the ankles.*
4. *Inhale diaphragmatically while stretching your toes outward so that they point in the same direction that your legs do.*
5. *Repeat 3 and 4 as much as desired. You should feel a wonderful massage in your ankles.*

6. *Lie down with arms to the side. Breathe through the nose. Relax and process the feelings in your body.*

Heat Massage

1. *Place hands in prayer position, palms facing each other in front of your chest. Rub palms together as hard and as fast as possible. Generate a lot of heat in your hands.*
2. *Place the palms over the eyes. Relax your hands, "merging" them with your eyes. Relax into the heat and magnetism from your hands, absorbing it into your eyes. You are breathing with the diaphragm through the nose. If you see "inner light" in the forehead, then relax into it, embracing it.*
3. *Massage around your eye sockets. Work your massage toward the back of your head. Massage all this energy all the way down your body; neck, torso, butt, legs, ankles and finally into the Earth. Feel or see the energy entering the Earth. Make sure you feel the "buzz" in your body by massaging with a lot of pressure.*
4. *Place your hands in prayer position, just like Mother Mary – palms together in front of the chest. Take three diaphragmatic breaths, **softening** into each breath **and deepening** your experience while feeling the new sensations in the body. Process these feelings fully.*
5. *Repeat step 1. Then, place palms over your ears. Listen to your pulse, breath and any inner sounds you may hear. Absorb the energy and massage downward, into the Earth.*
6. *Repeat step 4.*
7. *Repeat the whole process, but place your hands on the top of your head, right hand first and left hand on top of*

that. Whatever your "giving" hand is, that is the one that is touching your head.

8. Repeat step 4.
9. Do the same with hands on your heart, right hand on heart with left palm on the back of your other hand.
10. Repeat step 4.

You can make this one a "hot" exercise. Take a long, fast inhale when you're rubbing your hands together. Imagine looking straight ahead at a candle an arm's length in front of you. Blow out your candle like you have one birthday wish and only one blow to get that wish. The exhale should be complete, loud, extremely fast and coming from your mouth. Do this three times while rubbing the hands together before placing your hands on your body for the rest of the process.

You are getting your stagnant energy moving while generating heat. All contraindications from the introduction apply to the "hot" version of this exercise.

Core Awareness Exercise

Awareness of our "core" is a wonderful grounding element in any routine. The core is also essential for orienting ourselves to the rest of the world and establishing our unique identities.

1. Lie down on your back with arms at your sides.

2. Lift your legs so that they point straight up. You can bend your knees first and do it in stages if you wish.

3. Point your toes straight up. Pull your heels toward your head and your toes forward.

4. *Inhale diaphragmatically while performing step three. Also at the same time, contract your perineum (the area between the anus and genitals) and sphincter muscles by pulling them back toward the spine. Males will feel like they're holding back a pee.*

5. *Swallow with a loud gulp and exhale through the nose while lowering the legs to the ground and gradually relaxing your perineum. You are back in your original position.*

6. *Repeat a few times, remain on back, breathe and process the feelings in your body.*

Breath of Fire

The Breath of Fire is a "hot" pranayama exercise. All contraindications apply. This would be added to the breath section if it did not fit better with the muscle exercises in a warm up sequence.

The Breath of Fire quickly oxygenates all the organs of the body while synchronizing them all. It will enhance any other exercise that you do it with. For example, if you do the Breath of Fire before Tai Chi Chuan, it will enhance the benefits of Tai Chi Chuan.

You will feel this exercise very strongly at the point on the spine directly in back of the Navel Tan Tien. The breath should be very loud.

1. *Place your dominant hand on your chest and your nondominant hand on your belly. This is to make sure that your belly moves and your chest does not.*

2. *This breath is going to rate about one second per cycle. That is, a complete inhale and a complete exhale combined should take about one second.*
3. *Without moving your chest, inhale completely, puffing your belly out. Exhale completely, emptying your lungs. One second has passed. Repeat this 10 million times (or as many as comfortable). The inhale and exhale should be "equal" in force, volume and length. Filling up and emptying are both as quick as possible, like a pump or a toilet plunger.*
4. *Your belly is like a "pump". It will feel like your belly is pumping itself. Remember, your chest is not moving.*
5. *You fill feel your breath closer to the spine and lower neck than the inside of the nose. This is not a nasal sounding breath. The sound may come from the back of the nasal cavity, but pretend it's coming from the lower neck. You will be even more conscious of the breath in your belly, your center of focus.*
6. *Place your hands in prayer position, just like Mother Mary – palms together in front of the chest. Take three diaphragmatic breaths, **softening** into each breath **and deepening** your experience while feeling the new sensations in the body. Process these feelings fully.*

Belly Bounce

The belly bounce is a hot exercise.

1. *Stand with feet about a shoulder width apart.*
2. *Place your fingers and palms of both hands on your Navel Tan Tien, about 2 inches below the navel. The fingers of both hands are pointing to each other.*

3. *Bounce up and down without lifting your feet. Let your fingers and palms bounce up and down, too, massaging your belly. Your legs are like a spring with feet firmly on the ground. Exhale however you wish and as loud as you wish. It is best to inhale through your nose.*

4. *Place your hands in prayer position, just like Mother Mary – palms together in front of the chest. Take three diaphragmatic breaths, **softening and deepening** into each breath while feeling the new sensations in the body. Process these feelings fully.*

The Belly Bounce stirs up the belly chi and gathers chi to your belly.

Slapping and Wiping

This is another hot exercise.

1. *Briskly wipe your arms on the top and bottom so that you feel the buzz afterwards. Rapidly do the same for the tops of each hand and wrist.*

2. *Slap your chest rapidly near the thalamus. Slap your heart chakra rapidly between the nipples. While doing this, exhale through the mouth as if you're whispering "haaaaaaa". Inhale through the nose.*

3. *Slap your whole body all the way down the legs. Do not slap your kidneys (under and below the ribs in the back). Kidney injuries are not fun. Finish by wiping your legs.*

4. *Place your hands in prayer position, just like Mother Mary – palms together in front of the chest. Take three diaphragmatic breaths, **softening** into each breath **and deepening** your experience while feeling the new sensations in the body. Process these feelings fully.*

Ploughing the Thighs

Ploughing the Thighs is great for grounding and sudden concentration.

1. *Sit with your back straight and vertebrae stacked all the way up. Eyes look straight ahead.*
2. *Inhale diaphragmatically. Be mindful of the river of air as it enters your body. Enjoy the feelings of your body. You can close your eyes for the inhale if that helps. The heels of your hands are at the very top of your thighs at the pelvis end.*
3. *Exhale with a powerful but whispered "Ha" sound while "ploughing" the tops of your thighs all the way to knee and past it using the heel of your hand. You are pushing very hard so that your thighs tingle afterward from increased blood blow. The forward push is very fast to produce heat and friction.*
4. *Repeat the plow 6 or 7 times during this exhale. Feel the burn.*
5. *Place the heels of the hands in their original position and repeat the whole process.*
6. *Place your hands in prayer position, just like Mother Mary – palms together in front of the chest. Take three diaphragmatic breaths, **softening** into each breath **and deepening** your experience while feeling the new sensations in the body. Process these feelings fully.*

Gather Chi into your Navel Tan Tien

This exercise re-centers your energy to where it is safely stored. Some meditations involving the upper chakras can overheat the brain. This gift from Taoism is great after any meditation practice session and/or as a grounding warm up. Try it especially after working with meditations involving your upper chakras or when you feel spacey (if you feel spacey, try performing this exercise after massaging your head and neck and scratching your scalp).

As long as the pressure is light, there are no contraindications for this.

1. *Place a palm (men left palm and women right palm) on the Tan Tien with the other palm on top of that hand. Circle counterclockwise with very small circles. Counterclockwise in this case means that you are moving to the left at the bottom of the circle and to the right at the top of the circle). Do not push hard. Do this just enough to warm the skin. Don't worry. The grounding feeling will linger even with a very light pressure.*

2. *Gradually enlarge the circles. The circumference of the 18th circle should go through the solar plexus (soft spot just below junction of bottom two ribs in front of body).*

3. *Stop at the solar plexus. Reverse direction. Circles will gradually get smaller.*

4. *The 18th circle will be the smallest.*

5.   *Relax and enter yourself in the navel Tan Tien, your center of gravity. Feel the sensations in your body and pay attention to how you're breathing. Feel where you are still tense. Relax the tension using any method you wish. You may benefit by just breathing into the tense areas and relaxing them.*

Self Massage

The massage exercise is a long version. You can shorten it as much as you wish. Massage is a wonderful and loving part of every warm up. It is an excellent grounding exercise. Qigong practitioners often massage after meditating to disperse stagnant energy in the body and to get it flowing properly.

1.   *Begin with the Heat Massage exercise above.*

2.   *Vigorously scratch your whole scalp.*

3.   *Point your index fingers or thumbs, near the corners of your eyes by the nose. Make circles around the eyes in both directions, massaging the eye sockets.*

4.   *Come to the temples from the outer corners of the eyes. Massage the temples in circles.*

5.   *Place your index fingers at the center of your forehead. Push hard and pull your fingers apart toward the temples.*

6.   *Massage your temples in circles using your fingers again.*

7. *Massage all the soft indents around the ears. Pull on your ears with index finger and thumb until your whole ear is massaged.*

8. *Press hard on your cheek bones with your palms. Push along the cheek bones toward your ears.*

9. *Put fingers on each side of the nose. Push hard and pull down toward your mouth.*

10. *Place your fingers just under the flap between the nostrils. Find the pressure point and push into it. Pull toward your cheeks. It is like drawing a mustache.*

11. *Do the same in the indent between the lips and the chin.*

12. *Massage with circular movements all along the jaw bones.*

13. *Massage with circular movements the indents at the top of the neck where it meets the head. Avoid the spine, but get around the spine.*

14. *Put a thumb on either side of the spine at the top of the neck. Pull down, loosening the spine while avoiding the spine. Push hard.*

15. *Knead, with both hands and fingers, the muscles in the shoulders and upper back.*

16. *Knead all the muscles in the upper and lower arms.*

17. *Pull each finger of one hand with the fingers of the other hand. From the center of the palm, run your thumbs along each groove, following the groove toward the space between the fingers.*

18. Massage the center of each palm with your thumb.

19. Place fingers on either side of spine. Run your fingers along the spine without pushing on the spine itself. Do this for as much of the spine as possible.

20. Place fingers between the ribs at the top of the chest. Push hard and bring them toward the heart chakra.

21. Run your fingers down the grooves between the ribs, starting from the center of the chest.

22. Use any part of your hands for this. Inhale. Place fingers of both hands just under the ribs. While exhaling, massage along the bottom of the bottom ribs by pulling your hands apart, ending at your sides.

23. Do the same thing an inch below the last one.

24. A little lower.

25. A little lower.

26. Massage the waistline.

27. Make fists. Massage your kidneys with circular motions using the thumb and forefinger end of each fist. Make circles in both directions.

28. With your thumbs, massage your lower back from just next to the spine to the sides. You are pulling horizontally from your spine to your sides. Push hard. Begin as close as possible to your spine without pushing on it.

29. *Use your thumbs in circular motions to massage the entire groin and upper thigh area.*

30. *Work your way down to your knees. Knead the legs.*

31. *Circle, with your thumbs, inside the kneecap. Try to massage underneath the kneecap as much as possible without hurting it.*

32. *Massage behind the knee.*

33. *Work your way down the calves, shins and ankles.*

34. *Work the pressure points at the top of your foot. Run your thumbs down the grooves and toward the toes.*

35. *Gently pull each toe.*

36. *Hold a foot with both hands. Massage the bottoms of the feet with your thumbs.*

37. *If you wish to gather chi into your navel, you can try that exercise at the end.*

38. *Enjoy the relaxed throbbing feeling.*

Energy and Nature Exercises

Gathering Chi

This chi gathering technique is very similar to some Qigong practices for "gathering chi from heaven and Earth". Most Qigong versions of this use more continuous movements. This one uses massage for grounding the gathered energy.

1. *Begin in standing posture. Retain the inward awareness from the standing posture in this exercise. Be mindful of the Earth below you and the sky above you.*

2. *Place hands in prayer position. Take three breaths while relaxing and centering into each breath.*

3. *Point fingers down. Bring them to just above the ground with palms still together and knees slightly bent.*

4. *Move your hands away from and toward each other while relaxing the hands into Mother Earth. Try to feel the Earth's energy as you go along. Gather energy from the Earth. You may visualize this if you haven't developed your sensitivity yet.*

5. *Scoop up the Earth's magma into your hands.*

6. *Face your palms up with the back of your right hand resting on your left palm like you're holding a prescious gift.*

7. *Return to standing position and put the magma to your heart. Relax and absorb the Earth's magma.*

8. *Massage your chest and back. Massage all the way down to your legs and feet with the intent of bringing the energy all the way down into the Earth.*

9. *Return to standing and take three breaths in prayer position while checking the feelings in your body. Relax into each breath.*

10. *Point fingers forward and extend your arms forward with palms still together.*

11. *Pull your hands apart and push them back together again with the intent of gathering energy from the natural world in front of you. Perhaps it is a tree or a mountain or something you can't directly see because you are indoors. You may do this a few times.*

12. *Cup the energy with the back of your right hand resting against your left palm. Bring it to your heart. Relax and absorb.*

13. *Massage it down into the Earth.*

14. *Prayer position. Three breaths.*

15. *Push hands straight upwards above the head. They are still together with fingers pointing upward.*

16. *Look up. Gather chi from the sky.*

17. *Bring it to the top of your head. Right palm is on your head with left hand on top.*

18. *Relax and absorb.*

19. *Massage it all the way down into the Earth.*

20. *Prayer position. Three breaths.*

21. *Bring hands up again, over the head, while keeping palms together and fingers pointing up.*

22. *Turn your hands so that the backs of the hands are touching each other.*

23. *Push your hands out to your sides in a big circle. You are gathering chi from infinite galaxies. When they are outstretched to the sides (perpendicular to the ground), you are gathering chi from nature.*

24. *Bend down, completing the circle near the Earth. Now, you are gathering energy from the Earth again. There is a big soup of galaxy essence, nature essence and Earth essence in your hands. Grab the Earth's magma again and bring it back up to your heart.*

25. *Absorb this mixture of energy and massage it downward.*

26. *Prayer position.*

If you would like to synchronize this exercise with your breath, then remember the following principle:

The inhale corresponds to upward, outward, outstretching and expanding movements. The exhale corresponds to inward, downward, returning and contracting movements. For example, palms separate on the inhale and return together on the exhale.

Glowing Skeleton

This exercise helps to increase internal power. Try to imagine yourself feeling and seeing the energy and light. Over time, the visualization aspect of this will sharpen until you know you're working with real energy.

As you build your internal power, be careful not to confuse this with spiritual progress as many often do. Power trips can result from this. Remember that Darth Vader was also successful in cultivating his inner power. We can recklessly play with energy all we want, but always remember this: **Spirit is not energy**.

1. *Perform the standing posture exercise from the posture section. Connect with the natural environment. If you're indoors, "extend" your consciousness into the outdoors as well as the Earth and sky. Connect with love and smiles.*
2. *Inhale fully (always through your nose) and breathe light and energy from the elements into your feet and ankles. Just imagine this if you don't feel it yet.*
3. *Hold your breath. Clench your feet and ankles. Compress the light into the center of the bones in your feet and ankles.*
4. *Exhale while gradually releasing the muscles. Feel the difference.*
5. *Repeat the process for the legs. Clench first the calves and then the thighs. Compress that energy into the center of the bones.*
6. *Repeat for the hips.*
7. *Repeat for the torso. When clenching, first clench the lower abdomen, then the upper abdomen. Remember the spine and ribs.*
8. *Repeat for the arms and hands.*
9. *Repeat for the shoulders.*
10. *You're remembering the spine, right?*
11. *Repeat for the neck.*

12. *Repeat for the head. Clench those jaw muscles and forehead.*
13. *Place your hands in prayer position and bow to the elements.*
14. *Lovingly thank the elements for providing you with healing energy.*
15. *Close your eyes. Continue to breathe diaphragmatically while imagining your whole skeleton to be glowing. Using your inner vision, start your scan with your feet and legs and work your way up to the skull. Remember the spine. It's glowing, too. Then, jump out of yourself and look at your whole skeleton.*

Condensing Breath

The Condensing Breath is another gift from the Taoists. Condensing Breath cultivates internal power. It is not in the Pranayama section because it is better in the energy cultivation portion of a sequence. Notice the similarities to Glowing Skeleton.

1. *Perform the entire standing posture or the sitting posture exercise.*

2. *Breathe diaphragmatically, paying particular attention to your navel center.*

3. *Inhale and imagine the breath going into the bones of your arms. Pay no attention to the muscles and tissues. They don't exist. On each inhale, imagine the breath entering the arms from all directions and compressing the bones inward toward the marrow.*

4. *Do the same for the hands and fingers, then for the whole body one part at a time.*

5. *Place hands in prayer position. Take three long breaths, relaxing into each breath. Process the new feelings in the body.*

Inner Fire

Need fire in the belly? The inner fire ignites internal power. It is very energizing and recommended for the first phase of a warm-up. The breath should be deep, steady and through the nose. Keep the inhale and exhale even in "force", volume and length.

1. *Have a good belly laugh. Visualize the late Michael Jackson's monkey. That's the spirit. Laugh! Ha Ha Ha! What's the monkey wearing?*
2. *Rub your belly in a circular manner with one palm.*
3. *Imagine a small fire with hot embers in your belly.*
4. *Inhale. Imagine the breath blowing on the embers in your belly when it enters. Imagine what that sounds like.*
5. *Exhale a roaring fire to all the extremities of your body from the belly. The fire originates in your belly. Let the fire burn all your impurities.*
6. *Repeat.*
7. *Place your hands in prayer position, just like Mother Mary – palms together in front of the chest. Take three diaphragmatic breaths, **softening** into each breath **and deepening** your experience while feeling the new sensations in the body. Process these feelings fully.*

Earth Scan Preliminary Exercise

The preliminary exercise will train you how to move in a way that is guided by the inner muscles. Tai Chi masters use their inner muscles in their movements.

1. *Stand in the standing posture with arms to the sides, palms facing backwards.*
2. *Push your hands forward and upward until hands are at the level of the shoulder, fingers pointing straight ahead. Imagine you are pushing through water. At the top, the elbows may be very slightly bent with arms almost fully extended.*
3. *Bring the hands straight down the same way they came. The up and down movements should be one continuous motion. Imagine your center of gravity (navel center) as the originator of every movement. It all comes from the navel center.*
4. *Find a wall. Stand against the wall with arms down and palms facing backward. The whole front of your body, including the backs of the hands, is touching the wall.*
5. *Push with the backs of your hands as hard as you can into the wall. Push for 30 seconds.*
6. *Release and push for 30 more seconds.*
7. *Do this six or seven times.*
8. *Try steps 1 through 3 again. Your arms should lift up as if by themselves. You exhausted your superficial muscles so that the inner muscles took over. Remember what this feels like. This feeling is what you're aiming for with the Earth Scan.*
9. *Also try the Earth Scan before and after the wall exercise.*

Earth Scan

The Earth Scan is a sensitization exercise, especially for the hands and navel center. If you do not feel the Earth's energy, keep practicing. You will. The key is **softening and allowing a deeper experience**. The sensitization effect is cumulative over time as long as you practice it regularly. Otherwise, it's still a good meditation warm up.

1. *Stand in standing posture with arms to the sides and palms facing backwards. Do the complete standing posture exercise, including sensory orientation training. Remain conscious of the Earth below you and the sky above you.*
2. *Push forward and up with the backs of your hands until your hands are at the level of the solar plexus (the soft spot just under the junction of the two bottom ribs in the front of the body). Elbows are slightly bent and fingers are pointing forward. The palms are facing downward.*
3. *Center yourself in the navel center. Relax your hands so that they are fully present with the magnetic field and energy field of the Earth.*
4. *Using your navel center, shift your body weight back and forth between left and right foot.*
5. *Allow your hands to move along with the weight shift. They can move in any direction that feels natural, except up or down. They should remain at the level of the solar plexus.*
6. *Soften the hands as you go. Feel the Earth's energy. Move your hands with the inner muscles as much as possible. Move slowly so that you can feel the*

*sensations in your hands as you go along. Imagine
that you are pushing them through water.*

7. *Always be conscious of the Earth below you and the
sky above you. Eyes are always looking inward and
outward from within.*

8. *At some point, your breath will naturally
synchronize with your movements. Enjoy the
meditation.*

9. *Place your hands in prayer position, just like Mother
Mary – palms together in front of the chest. Take
three diaphragmatic breaths, **softening** into each
breath **and deepening** your experience while feeling
the new sensations in the body. Process these
feelings fully.*

There is another step you can add to this. Once in a while,
cross the right hand over the left. Hold the right hand over the left
and feel the magnetic interaction between the hands. Turn your
palms up and feel the sensations. Turn them back down and
continue the movements. Try this also with the left hand over the
right hand.

More Hand Sensitization Exercises

To deepen your sensitivity, you may rub your hands
together vigorously before each of these hand exercises. This will
stimulate the chakras in the center of your palms.

1. *Rub your palms together vigorously and generate heat.
Place them in prayer position. Pull your palms at least
12 inches apart and slowly bring them back together
while noticing any sensations and interactions between*

the two palms. You are compressing energy. Repeat many times, softening the hands each time.

2. Place palms a half inch apart, facing each other. Move one palm in tiny circles and gradually let the circles become larger. Switch direction once in awhile – first counterclockwise, then clockwise. Switch hands. Do this slowly enough so that you can feel the movement of the hands and the interactions between them. Soften into the exercise. You can try a variation of this one by gradually pulling the moving hand away from the other one as the circles gradually get larger.

3. If you have a partner, you can try the above exercises using their palms with yours. It is easier to feel someone else's energy.

4. Point your left palm up while it sits near your navel. Point your right middle finger downward into the center of the left palm. Stir the magma of the Earth with your right middle finger while feeling the sensations in the palms. You can allow the circles to gradually become larger. Do it counterclockwise and clockwise.

5. Turn your left arm and hand so that your wrist and palm are up. Place your right hand 2 inches from your shoulder. Very slowly "scan" your arm with your right palm, moving toward the tips of your left fingers. Notice any changes in feeling throughout the route; tingling, cold, heat, "nothingness", sudden twitches, pushing, pulling, etc. Reverse direction and make your way back to the shoulder. Switch hands. Eventually, as your sensitivity builds, you may successfully scan people and trees like this and from across the room.

6. Create an energy ball. Place your palms a few inches apart, facing each other. Imagine a ball of light between

*your hands. Play with it for awhile. Massage the
bottoms of your feet with it until you feel subtle
sensations of tingling, cold, heat, vibration, itching, etc.
Massage all your energy centers and wherever you feel
tense with this ball. Send it into the earth's core when
you are finished with it.*

Chi Cocktails

Energy follows thought. Form follows energy. Form also provides a channel for energy. Remember this when doing all energy techniques. The imagination brings real results when the mind is concentrated.

The following techniques will allow you to more easily receive beneficial energy from the elements while cultivating jing.

1. *Bathe in the sun's light. Help it along with your imagination by visualizing golden light showering your whole body, especially your head.*
2. *Drink the sun's light as if you're drinking through a straw. Suck it in through your partially closed mouth and let the energy mix with your saliva.*
3. *Hold the breath and contract the perineum and anus muscles, pulling them up toward your abdomen. Men should feel like they're holding back a pee.*
4. *Swallow with a gulping sound. Let the energy drop down like food as you exhale through the nose and gradually relax the perineum. Men should stop the exhale when it drops into the testicles. Women should stop the exhale when it drops into the point between the ovaries.*

5. You can do this exercise with the moon (imagine a silver light) and the twilight (before sunrise or after sunset).

Kinesthetic Exercise for Concentration and Focusing Chi

You can try this exercise if you feel spacey or unfocused. It also seems to unite head and heart.

1. You can sit or stand, but keep the back straight and the nose pointing straight ahead with vertebrae stacked properly. Eyes can be open or closed. Try both.
2. Put your right thumb and forefinger together like you're giving the "OK" sign. Keep the remaining three fingers as straight as possible without strain and pointing up.
3. Palm is forward in front of your shoulder at shoulder height.
4. Inhale diaphragmatically.
5. Your exhale is a "shhhhhhhhhh" sound. You can play with the sound my moving your lips around in funny ways.
6. During the exhale, you are pushing your palm forward like you are pushing through water. You are keenly aware of all the subtle changes and feelings in your arm and hand. Extend arm forward all the way, keeping palm facing forward.
7. Pivot your palm in a U-turn so that it faces you. Keep it at shoulder level. This transition should be as graceful as a fish in water.
8. Bring your palm back toward your shoulder. You are still making the "shhhhhhh" sound. Notice any energetic interplay between your hand and the side of your head.

9. When your palm is almost to your shoulder, make another U-turn and push the palm back out straight ahead.

10. Keep going back and forth. One entire cycle –forward and back – will probably be about 7 seconds. Go just slow enough so that you can feel everything that is happening.

11. You will run out of breath after a few cycles. Inhale through the nose, being mindful of the sensations in your body, and start over with "shhhhhhh".

12. As your awareness expands, you may expand your attention to the subtle feelings in the entire body but with a specific focus on the arms, wrist, hand and fingers.

13. Your experiments with the movement of your lips, over time, will become energetically synchronized with the movement of your hands. You will know it when this has occurred. This will happen sometime after you embrace step 12.

14. Another thing to be mindful of is the energy circuit caused by the closing of your thumb and index finger. You may feel an intense concentration of chi in that circuit.

Chakra Clearing

The following exercise will involve some active visualization and some passive visualization. Active content is what you consciously create. Passive content is what your subconscious or your intuition brings to you. With practice, passive visualization will symbolically reveal something that is actually going on inside you, like a "dirty", "depleted" or "over-energized" chakra, for instance.

You may wish to record yourself reading this slowly. Play it back to yourself and follow your instructions.

1. *Relax and take a few deep breaths with eyes closed.*
2. *You are a white ball of light, an orb, in the center of your chest between the nipples. Your consciousness is centered in this orb.*
3. *Move upward into your throat. Imagine the energy in your throat becoming calm and clear with your touch.*
4. *Go up to the point between the eyebrows and inward near the center of the brain. Allow the energy to clear and balance.*
5. *Go up to the soft spot at the top of your head.*
6. *Travel back down through all these points while gathering your body consciousness into your ball. Go down to your heart area again.*
7. *From your heart area, go down to the solar plexus and three inches inward, clearing and balancing with your touch.*
8. *Go to your navel center which is a couple inches below your navel and a couple inches in.*
9. *Go to the point behind and just above your pubic bone on the spine.*
10. *Go to your tailbone and perineum (sensitive area between the anus and genitals).*
11. *Go through your ankles, clearing any stagnation, and then through the bottoms of your feet.*
12. *Go a couple hundred feet into the Earth. Find a very large rock. Attach a chord from yourself to this rock. Make the chord and the connection strong.*

13. *Go up to your feet.*
14. *Go through the feet, ankles, perineum, the spot behind the pubic bone, the navel center, the solar plexus, the heart chakra, the throat chakra, the third eye chakra, up to the crown, the soft spot at the top of your head.*
15. *Go out your crown and three feet above your head. Look around.*
16. *Go upward, past the sun and moon, through thousands of galaxies.*
17. *Go past the end of the universe. You will see a blue-ish white light in the distance. Go toward that light.*
18. *The light is becoming bigger and bigger until it's right in front of you. Go into the light.*
19. *Immerse yourself in the light. It is the place where only Spirit resides. Your brainwaves are vibrating at a Theta frequency, the dream frequency, the frequency that spawned Einstein's ideas before he turned them into science. God is very responsive to people who enter this frequency. Come back later and ask any question you wish. You will get an answer. Let go and allow yourself to receive the answer at the right time. All things are possible.*
20. *Make a command, as co-creator of the universe, that God grant you open, aligned and integrated chakras. Have God do this in alignment with the highest good. Give thanks and acknowledge that the prayer is already granted.*
21. *Now, all you have to do is witness the granting of the prayer symbolically and it will come true.*
22. *Go back down to the universe, through the galaxies, past the sun and moon. Stop just above your head.*

23. *Enter the crown through the crown chakra.*
24. *Go through your whole body, clearing and balancing as you go. Through the third eye, the throat, the heart, the solar plexus, the navel, the pubus, the perineum, the ankles, the feet.*
25. *Go back up to the perineum and tailbone. Imagine a glass ball about the size of a tennis ball. What does it look like? Is it smaller than a tennis ball? Is it bigger? Are there dark spots? Is it dim? Are there murky spots? Chakras, in reality, spin like wheels, but that's not important unless you want it to be. You can imagine them stationary or spinning.*
26. *If it is not a bright shiny red and the size of a tennis ball, then witness it being showered by white light from the heavenly realm. Let the light push out dark spots. Let it brighten the ball if it's dim. Let it resize the ball if it is too big or too small. Let it polish the ball to give it a bright glowing color. This is not just your imagination. The process is really happening. God is doing the washing. Not you. You are just witnessing so that the prayer becomes true.*
27. *Move up to the place on the spine behind the pubic bone. This one should be a bright orange ball that is the size of a tennis ball. Repeat the showering process from step 26.*
28. *Go to the Navel center. This should be a bright yellow ball with a hint of orange.*
29. *Go to the solar plexus, a bright yellow ball with a hint of green.*
30. *Go to the heart chakra between the nipples. It should be bright green.*

31. *Go to the throat chakra. It should be aqua blue. If you are more emotional than logical, then make it a darker blue with less green (green is the heart color).*
32. *Go to the third eye chakra. It should be indigo.*
33. *Go to the crown chakra. It should be violet.*
34. *Go three feet above your head to the chakra associated with the soul. This is a light point of light.*
35. *Go back into your crown, down into your heart chakra and out the front of your heart chakra.*
36. *Look at yourself and all your chakras. See them in perfect balance.*
37. *Go back into your heart chakra, then up and out your crown.*
38. *Go back up to the place where only Spirit exists and give thanks.*

Notice the progression of colors. In a nutshell, it is ROY G BIV. That is, the rainbow colors; red, orange, yellow, green, blue, indigo, violet. The yellow navel chakra has an orange tinge because it is close to the orange chakra. The yellow solar plexus chakra has a green tinge because it is close to the green chakra (heart). Your throat chakra has a choice between greenish blue and darker blue depending on whether you want it to be more emotional (heart) or logical (third eye). If you're more emotional than logical, go for the darker blue. If you wish to keep this exercise simpler, then skip either the pubic chakra or the solar plexus and use Roy G Biv without the color blends. This will give you seven chakras – one for each color of the rainbow.

You can go back to the place where only God exists before any visualization exercise or prayer session and do the work in this space. It will enhance it greatly. Be sure to go into the Earth to ground yourself first before you go up.

You can visit this space to ask questions if you wish. After the question, relax, let go, daydream, jot your daydream on a piece of paper. You may get your answer on the paper or through direct knowingness, through a chance encounter with a stranger or through dream-type imagery. Don't force it. Let go.

When you enter this place before creative visualization work, stay up there and then begin the visualization exercise from this space.

Exercises for the Imagination

The last exercise in the Energy and Nature section brought you to the place where only God exists. Again, go there before any imagination exercise. Do your visualizations from that place of light. By the way, I would like to thank Vianna Stibal for bringing that space into the public mind again. Vianna's visualization for entering that space is more elaborate in order to create a more structured system for intuitive and healing work. Vianna's works can be found at www.thetahealing.com.

Black Box of Roses

The Box of Roses strengthens the imagination. As you develop the imagination, it will be increasingly necessary to learn how to dissipate energy. Blowing up the roses in the exercise is good practice for dissipation.

1. *Look into the black box on the next page. Picture a red rose. Visualize it as vividly as possible. Smell it. Feel its texture.*

2. *Examine the rose closely. Are there any wilted petals? Are the petals fully open or tight? What does the stem look like? Is it long? Is the rose wet like it was just watered? Any irregularities or brown spots? Bugs? Thorns?*

3. *Blow up the rose. Vaporize it.*

4. *Repeat steps 1-3 with roses of all colors of the rainbow; red, orange, yellow, green, blue, indigo, violet.*

Ocean

The ocean exercise is a combination between an imagination and a nature exercise. Your subconscious mind will not know the difference between an imaginary ocean and a real one. Record yourself reading this and play it back if you wish.

1. *Sit in sitting posture and enter a relaxed space.*

2. *In front of you is a trailhead with a sign that says "beach trails". What does the sign look like? What are you wearing? Are you carrying anything? Look at the vegetation. What kinds of trees are there? What types of grass? How green is the grass? Smell the distant ocean.*

3. *You are walking along the trail. Can you hear seagulls in the distance? Stop and look at the insects. Feel the ocean breeze and listen as it blows through the trees.*

4. *The trail is leading you out of the trees. The ocean sounds are suddenly louder. The wind is stronger.*

5. *You are no longer in the shade. The sun feels very warm on your skin. You come to a cliff which overlooks the ocean. The sun is straight ahead over the water. It is not long before sunset.*

6. *Take your shoes off. Walk around, enjoying the feeling of the sand between your toes. Sit down and enjoy your sunset. Feel the sand and wind. Smell the ocean. Listen to the ocean waves and seagulls. Feel your whole body relaxing into the beauty. Fast forward, if you wish, to enjoy the sunset sooner.*

Meet your Soul

The more you practice this exercise, the more "real" the experience becomes. The information you receive from this may totally amaze you the first time. You will gradually align yourself with the guidance from your soul. This one is great for practicing both active and passive visualization.

It is best to use the "going up" method in the Chakra Clearing exercise immediately before this visualization. It will greatly enhance the intuitive information you receive. Go up through your crown to the place where only Spirit exists and stay there during the following visualization.

1. *Enter a relaxed state of mind using your preferred method.*

2. *Imagine a portal of bluish-purple light in front of you. You are well aware that this portal takes you to anywhere you wish to go. Walk toward it and enter it.*

3. *You are exiting the portal into the most beautiful nature spot you've ever seen. Look around. Notice all the details. How does the place feel? Notice the smells and the wind, if any. Listen to any birds, insects or water. Explore this place for a while.*

4. *There is a large hole in the ground. You are expecting your soul to come out of that hole to pay you a visit. How large is it? Is it rocky or grassy?*

5. *Say a few prayers to prepare for a visit from your soul, your highest, wisest self. Burn sage or incense if you wish. You can also draw a circle or whatever feels right to you.*

6. *The soul is emerging from the hole. Don't try to guess what form your soul will take on. Just let it emerge.*

7. *Is your soul humanlike? Is it like a monster or an animal? Is it otherworldly? Look closely.*

8. *Bow to your soul and let it know that you are ready to receive its wisdom. You may ask specific questions if you like. Ask that you remember all the information.*

9. *Your soul may answer your questions by sending pictures, by speaking, through gestures or by directly transmitting information to you, perhaps in a beam of light. It may even draw pictures and hand them to you. You could receive a gift from your soul. Accept it. There*

is even a chance that it may get up and start dancing with an Uncle Sam hat and a flag that says "Star Spangled Funky" or something. Anything is possible.

10. *Be patient. Let go and allow the soul to communicate at its own pace.*

11. *When the process is complete, bow and thank your soul for its guidance.*

12. *When it seems right, open your eyes. Jot down EVERYTHING that you can remember onto a piece of paper – even the tiniest little details that seem totally ridiculous. They could be useful to you. Don't try to over-interpret. Absorb the information and perhaps your intuition will guide you further if it hasn't already.*

Ecstatic Waterfall of Light

Bathing in love is the theme of this one. It can be considered an emotional exercise, an imagination exercise or an energy and nature exercise.

1. *Close your eyes and relax in whatever way works best.*

2. *In front of you is your magic portal to anywhere you wish to go. It is a bluish-purple light. Enter it.*

3. *You are popping out of the portal, into the most beautiful, lush nature scene you've ever experienced. Look at the ground. Look at the trees. Feel the ground and the wind. Smell the fragrances of the flowers. Hear the river that is just out of sight. It does not sound like an ordinary river. It has a lighter quality.*

4. *As you walk toward the river, you notice that it is a river of white light. The light is the stuff that love is made of. There is a waterfall in front of you. Take off your clothing and walk toward it.*

5. *When you first step into the river, you will notice the pure ecstasy that it awakens in your feet. It is almost an erotic love, but very pure and divine. Tingles and shivers move all the way up and down your spine. You are overwhelmed by how ecstatic this light is.*

6. *By the time you get to the waterfall, the light will be up to your waste. It is absolutely shocking how good it feels.*

7. *Walk to the waterfall and bathe in it. Let it pour all over you, cleaning all the impurities in your body and mind until you are beaming with light, alert relaxation and ecstatic love. Scrub all your tense areas with this light.*

8. *Bathe as long as you wish.*

9. *Afterward, you can climb up the rocks to a flat ledge. You may sit and meditate or lie on your back. You realize that all your natural surroundings are one big sea of energy. Melt into that sea of energy, enjoying all the beauty within yourself.*

10. *Open your eyes.*

You can do this same exercise with a waterfall of rainbow colors. Trust that the right colors will go exactly where they are needed in your energy field. You can also do this exercise seven times, each with a different color of the rainbow. If you love Jesus meditations, imagine following the river upstream to its source: Jesus. Have a personal meeting. You can also do the same with your soul by combining this with the "Meet your Soul" exercise.

Grounding into Earth and Sky

This visualization seems to have come from Wiccan circles. However, every element within it is very common in the world of grounding visualizations. It is a multi-faceted, multi-purpose grounding visualization that is great for preparing for healing, magical work and meditation.

1. *Close your eyes and relax using your preferred method.*

2. *Keep your feet on the ground. It is preferable to start with the full Standing Posture exercise.*

3. *Imagine yourself growing roots from your feet, deep into the Earth. Let them grow until they reach the fiery core of the Earth.*

4. *A pressure is building in the Earth's core. Allow your roots to be open and receptive to receive this energy. You don't have to do anything to receive this energy. Just be open to it.*

5. *Let go of anything you wish to let go of (anger, tension, distracting thought, etc.) and send it into the core of the Earth to be burned up and transformed.*

6. *Let the energy fill you with light. Let it pass through the layers of the earth, through the soles of the feet, opening them, then through your genitals, belly, and all the way up.*

7. Allow this process to continue for awhile until you're really "full" like a stretched balloon. Your whole body is shining with light.

8. Let this light go to the sky and merge with the starlight. You are now open to the starlight.

9. Allow the starlight to pour through your branches, filling you with light. You are shining as bright as a star.

10. Let the starlight go through your roots and into the Earth, merging with the fiery core of the Earth.

11. Now, when you inhale through the nose, you are drawing that "energy soup" in through the roots and sending it up to the stars. On the exhales, you are bringing the energy back down, through you and into the Earth's core. Do this for a while.

12. Now, when you inhale, bring the Earth energy from the Earth to your heart and let it stop there. On the exhale, let the star energy come into your heart and stop there. Do this for a while.

13. Now, on the inhales, draw energy from both Earth and sky into your heart. On the exhales, imagine the energies mixing and swirling in your heart center. Do this a few times until you're warm and expanded.

14. Now, continue drawing from both Earth and sky on the inhales. On the exhales, let the energy travel from your heart to your hands. Your hands will eventually tingle, feel very warm and glow with light.

15. *Allow all excess energy to drain back through the roots and into the Earth's core until all jitteriness and manic feelings subside. A grounded and balanced feeling is what should remain.*

Exercises for the Intellect

The most obvious form of intellectual warm up is reading. You can read your favorite works that speak to the soul. This could mean scripture, poetry, spiritual writings, inspirational material – anything that brings you to a special place within. During a warm-up, you can spend just a couple minutes doing this until it begins to take effect. Some Contemplative Christians use this as the beginning of their warm-up program which is called the "Stepladder to Heaven".

If you love spiritual quotes from around the world, then you can visit my quotations website at www.angelfire.com/extreme/empoweringpeople. It is "a collection of quotes which point to the oneness of the experience of God in all traditions".

The pondering of spiritual concepts is a favorite exercise in the Buddhist world. The more you ponder, the more refined your "radio dial" becomes. The intellect ain't so bad or "unspiritual". In fact, it can help us.

Exercises for the Emotions

We will open this section with some insight into the anatomy of devotional singing. In devotional singing, the following tips are helpful.

Steps for effective chanting

1. *While singing, close your eyes and begin by pretending that your voice is coming from the bottom of your neck, in the back by your collar bone. Feel that spot vibrate. Let your voice begin with a somewhat "nasal" quality, but not completely nasal. In other words, you will feel it in the back and bottom of the nasal cavity, but not the entire nasal cavity.*

2. *Slow down your chant if you need to. There is probably an optimum speed for you in this moment.*

3. *Allow the vibrating feeling to include the top of your neck, in the back, where the neck meets the back of your head. Let that bottom bone in the back of your head feel it, too. Relax into the vibrations.*

4. *Relax into the chant and allow it to vibrate further down into your heart chakra. You will know when this occurs when you feel the chant originating in the stomach as well as the top and bottom of the throat. Your voice should "expand" and become less nasal.*

5. *Relax further. You will notice a circuit being created both up and down your entire spine. Your third eye may open up. Look up into your third eye and keep looking there. Smile into your third eye if you wish. See the*

whole body with the third eye while still focusing on the chant. Relax into the chant.

6. *If you're really cookin', your Petuitary gland may secrete a hormone called Amrita (Ahm-ree'-tuh, Sanskrit for nectar). Your saliva will taste sweeter and you may feel an electrified feeling in your palette and tongue. Swallowing your saliva will lead to blissful sensations of unconditional love in your heart. The Taoists think of this secretion as the longevity potion and some people call it the Fountain of Youth.*

7. *If the song is in a different language, such as Sanskrit, keep the translation in mind so that you know what you are singing for.*

8. *Remain inwardly oriented and stay focused on the deity or aspect of Spirit that you are singing to. The inward awareness will make it apparent that you are not singing to anything outside of yourself. A deity is an aspect of God. Those who mistake a deity for something outside of themselves often tend to get caught up in the mistaken belief systems called Polytheism and fundamentalist Monotheism. The worship of graven images do not help us any. If anything, it divides people. This graven image worship includes gurus. A guru is a mirror of what's already inside you.*

9. *You may be conscious of your whole body during chant. It may seem like your third eye and crown are gazing at everything, filling your whole body with light. In the New Testament, it says "when thy eye be single, thy whole body shall be full of light."*

10. *End the chant by gradually slowing it down and fading it into silence. Then, repeat it silently. All sounds dissolve into silence. When you incorporate this principle into your practice, you are reminding yourself of the nature of Spirit, which is all-expansive silence.*

11. *Chanting can become a meditation in itself. If you slip into a meditative state, stay with it without attachment. Be the loving detached observer.*

This seems a little mechanical, doesn't it? Guaranteed, chanting becomes LESS mechanical and more heart centered if you follow these steps. You're efforting into effortlessness. You don't just "be effortless" because it requires too much effort to "be effortless" and to "just be" for that matter. The mechanical steps in the above tips will eventually just fall apart until you are left with nothing but effortlessness.

We all love to be "right-brained". Why would we only want to use half of our being? Is it because the schools taught us to be left brained? Does that make half of your being evil?

Sanskrit Chants

Ganesh: elephant god, remover of obstacles, son of Shiva and Parvati. Imagine an elephant running through the forest, taking out all the obstacles in the way. Ganesh chants are a great beginning for any kirtan (devotional chanting session in Sanskrit). Remember, a deity is an aspect of the One. Ganesha is a name or a face of god.

Ganesh Mantra

Om gan ganapataye namaha
(Salutations to Ganesha with surrender and love)

Pronunciation: Ohm gahng gah-nah-pah-tah-yay' nah'-mah-hah

Ganesha Sharanam

Ganesha sharanam, sharanam Ganesha   *(Refuge in Ganesha)*

Ganesha sharanam, sharanam Ganesha   *(Refuge in Ganesha)*

Gan Gan Ganapati   *(Gan is a seed syllable. Ganapati means "Lord of the Group")*

Sharanam Ganesha

Gan Gan Ganapati

Sharanam Ganesha

Om gan ganapataye namaha   *(namaha means "I release this prayer energy with surrender and love".)*

Pronunciation: Guh-nesh'-uh shah'-rah-nahm, gung gung gah'- nuh-pah'-tee

Durga and Kali: Two aspects of the Divine Mother. Both are the face of Pure Love. However, Kali is usually more ferocious looking. She has many arms and wears the skulls of demons around her neck. She is a great protector and deals with elements of destruction and purification. Offer up your inner demons to her. Remind her to be gentle by saying "badra Kali" (pronounced bah'-drah Kah'-lee) or "Gentle, Kali".

Chamundaye Kali Ma   *(I offer you all my unneeded baggage, Mother Kali)*

Kali Ma Kali Ma Kali Ma   *(Mother Kali)*

Pronunciation: shah-moon'-die (rhymes with pie)-yay Kah-lee mah

Durge Durge   *(door'-gay door'-gay)* [translation: Durga Durga]

Durge jai jai Ma   *(door'-gay jay jay mah) [all power to Durga]*

Repeat the above four times.

Karuna sagari Ma   *(kah-roon'-uh sah'-gah-ree mah) [ocean (sagari) of compassion (karuna)]*

Karuna sagari Ma

Kali kapalini Ma   *(kah'-lee kah-pah'-lee-nee [otherwise, kah'-pah-lee-nee mah) [Mother Kali skull girl]*

Kali kapalini Ma

Jhagado dharini Ma   *(jug'-uh-do dah'-ree-nee mah) [realize the presence of the Goddess]*

Jhagado dharini Ma

Jagatambe jai jai ma   *(jug-uh-dum'-bay jay jay mah) [Mother Goddess of the Universe, all power to her]*

Shiva

Shiva means "auspicious one". He is transcendent and untouched by illusion. When in motion, he is "Nataraja" or "Lord of the Dance" and grows many arms. Shiva is in charge of destruction and transformation and plays the "Damaru" (dah'-muh-roo) drum. The music from the drum is the heartbeat of the universe. When you get to know Shiva, you do not "know Shiva". You "are Shiva".

Mantra:

Om Namah shivaya *(ohm nah-mah' shee-vie'[rhymes with pie]-ya*

Hanuman

Hanuman is the monkey god mentioned elsewhere in this book. He is pure devotion.

Mantra:

Mangala Murti *(mahn'-gahl-uh moo'-rah-tee)*

Maruta Nandana *(mah'-roo-tuh nahn'-dah-nah)*

Shakala Amangala *(shah'-kah-lah uh-mung'-gah-lah)*

Mulani Kandana *(moo'-lah-nee kun'-dah-nuh)*

Translation: Son of the wind, you are the embodiment of happiness. You remove all suffering at its root.

Radha and Krishna

Radha and Krishna are the two lovers. Govinda is a name of Krishna. They represent lover and Beloved and the inner marriage of yin and yang, humanity and Spirit.

Radhe Govinda

Radhe Radhe   *(Rahd'-hay Rahd'-hay)*

Radhe Govinda   *(Rahd'-hay Goh-vin'-duh)*

Spirit and Nature

Spirit and nature

Dancing together

Spirit and nature

Dancing together

Radhe Radhe

Radhe Govinda Jaya   *(Rahd'-hay Goh-vin'-duh*
Jie'[rhymes with pie]-ya)

Radhe Radhe

Radhe Govinda Jaya

For more Sanskrit chants, you can Google more songs with the keywords, Kirtan (keer'-tahn), devotional chant and bhajan (buh'-jin).

The River is Flowing (Wiccan Chant)

The river is flowing

Flowing and growing

The river is flowing

Back to the sea

Mother carry me

Your child I will always be

Mother carry me

Back to the sea

We are Opening (Wiccan Chant)

We are opening up in sweet surrender

To the luminous love light of the One.

(Repeat all this again)

We are opening

We are opening

We are opening

We are opening

Yeshua Alaha (Aramaic Jesus Chant)

Yeshua Alaha   *(Yeh'-shoo-uh All'-uh-hah)*
[Jesus God]

Note: Jesus' full first name was Yehoshua (Yeh-hoe'-shoo-uh). A shorter version is Yeshua. The shortest Aramaic version was Eshu (Eh'-shoo or Ay'-shoo or somewhere in between).

John Lennon Chant

All you need is love

All you need is love

All you need is love love

Love is all you need

On and on it goes. Just make something up that is meaningful for you.

Lovingkindness (Metta)

The Goenka School of Vipassana teaches one primary warm-up method which is to be performed before Mindfulness Meditation (Vipassana) and, in some cases, afterward. The warm-up method is called "Metta", which means compassion.

When we let go of grudges and harmful interpersonal dynamics, we cultivate peace in ourselves. Meditation becomes much easier when we turn this into a formal process. Metta is excellent near the end of a warm-up sequence.

Vipassana practitioners often cultivate their Metta throughout the day. They say that a well developed Metta practice brings powerful transformations within everyone you interact with. It also develops concentration which depends on feelings of love.

If compassion exercises make you uncomfortable with feelings of anger, inadequacy, etc, great! Do it more! You're efficiently working through your garbage.

The three exercises here are placed so that visual, kinesthetic and auditory learners all have a pool of techniques to choose from.

Global Smile

1. *Sit or stand with eyes closed.*

2. *Begin with yourself. Perform a complete inner smile cycle. Bathe in the peace.*

3. *Inhale and honor yourself. Do this for every inhale from here on in.*

4. *On the exhales, imagine yourself smiling at your neighbors – all of them. Imagine their faces glowing with light as all their tension is lifted.*

5. *After awhile, think of people whom you feel have harmed you in the past. Beam them each a few smiles and watch their tension transform into love.*

6. *Beam more smiles to your whole town or city*

7. *Beam smiles to the whole nation, the whole continent, the whole earth, and then everything beyond that plus all sentient beings in the heavenly realms (You don't have to believe in them. If they do exist, they'll appreciate it very much.).*

Spoken Metta

1. *Begin with a complete inner smile.*

2. *Recite the following:*

May I experience the highest happiness

May all people experience the highest happiness

May all sentient beings experience the highest happiness

May all sentient beings be free from suffering

The purest love surrounds all things

May we all taste this sweet nectar

3. *You may do this four times, facing the four directions. If you're ambitious, you can cover everyone in the heavens and ethers, above and below, for a total of six directions.*

4. *Name names; people you love, people you can't stand. Feel them being liberated from suffering with compassion. Send forgiveness to those who you are resentful toward. Send out prayers of peace.*

5. *Visualize all these actions having real effects on specific people and on entire societies. You really are influencing the world in ways that you cannot see.*

Or something like that. Smile upon your brother! Feel the love, brothas and sistas!

Radiant Light

1. *Perform the whole Standing Posture sequence.*

2. *Bend your knees in slow motion while focusing on your Hara (Navel Tan Tien). Move your butt up and down*

while bending your knees accordingly. Relax into your Hara (hah'-rah). Return to Standing Posture with knees slightly bent.

3. *On the inhale, visualize God's light entering your crown and swirling into your Hara.*

4. *On the exhale, imagine the energy continuing to swirl into your Hara.*

5. *Perform steps 3 and 4 with greater and greater intensity until your "cup runneth over".*

6. *Exhale energy from your Hara into the rest of your body, filling every cell with radiant light. Do the same specifically for your hands and feet.*

7. *Inhale and imagine more light coming in from the crown and into your Hara.*

8. *Repeat steps 6 and 7 with greater and greater intensity until satisfied.*

9. *You can try an optional variation of this. While inhaling, place your right palm on your Hara with the left palm covering it. When you exhale, bring the hands forward, separating them and gradually bring them to just in front of your shoulders. Your palms are forward, your fingers pointing straight up and your elbows pointing down. Your forearms are vertical. If you've ever been robbed at gunpoint, you know what I mean. On the next inhale, gradually bring the hands back to the Hara.*

10. *Now, when you exhale, you are radiating the light from your Hara to your enemies while knowing that you are*

intimately connected with the whole universe. They become lighter and happier.

11. *Do the same for your family, your neighborhood, your workplace, city, state, nation, planet, the celestial realms and all sentient beings.*

Breath Exercises

Who is God? He is the breath inside the breath. — Kabir

For all practical purposes, breath equals awareness. The deeper the breath, the more feeling you experience. The ancient Hebrew word ruah meant "the breath of life" or the breath inside the breath. So does prana in the Sanskrit language. Tuning into the breath brings greater control of the internal energy and internal power. It also stills the prana and therefore the agitated mind.

Pranayama means the control and stilling of prana. As you do these exercises, keep in mind that breathing is not pranayama. Breathing is the gateway to pranayama. The stilling of prana is essential for the perception of Spirit.

You have already learned some wonderful breathing techniques in this book. The following two exercises are perfect for the end of a warm up sequence before practicing meditation. They are great followed by "Om Shanti Shanti Shanti" (ohm shahn'-tee, Divine Peace) while looking into the forehead.

Alternate Nostril Breathing Pranayama

Alternate Nostril Breathing creates balance in both the brain and the chakras and oxygenates the whole body while purifying the chakras. It is calming and produces a grounded and balanced state that is conducive for deep meditation.

Make sure your inhales and exhales are equal in volume, length and strength. Do not force the breath. The more relaxed you are, the more correctly you are breathing. Relax into the breath and soon you will be doing it right.

1. *Pull your chin down and back a little bit toward the neck. The crown is being pulled up as with an imaginary string. This creates a valve or a "throat lock" which allows energy to move vertically in the spine without leakage. Stack your vertebrae. Your nose points straight ahead or slightly down.*

2. *Place your right index and middle finger at the point between your eyebrows. Place your ring finger on the side of your left nostril, ready to close it. Place your thumb on the side of your right nostril, ready to close it. Look into your forehead if you wish.*

3. *Breathe in and out a few times.*

4. *Cover the right nostril and exhale completely through the left nostril.*

5. *Relax the abdomen.*

6. *Inhale completely through the left nostril.*

7. *Close the left nostril and exhale completely through the right nostril.*

8. *Relax the abdomen.*

9. *Inhale completely through the right nostril.*

10. *Cover the right nostril and exhale completely through the left nostril.*

11. *Relax the abdomen.*

12. *Inhale completely through the left nostril.*

13. *Keep going in this same cycle.*

If you wish to practice breath retention (kumbhaka) then you will oxygenate your system more thoroughly. At the end of both the inhale and the exhale, hold the breath for roughly half the length of an inhale or an exhale. You may count to 8 on an inhale, hold for a 4 count, then exhale for an 8 count. When doing this, take full note of the feeling of stillness in the retention. There are contraindications for kumbhaka. If you are not relatively healthy, consult your doc.

Ujjayi Pranayama and Chi Circulation – Beginning and Advanced

Ujjayi (pronounced "oot – jie '[rhymes with "pie"] – yee" or "oo – jie' – yee" or at least something close to these depending on dialect) is the author's personal favorite pranayama. Ujjayi Pranayama ushers a profound meditative state, oxygenates the blood and balances the male and female energies.

The advanced form of Ujjayi described below is very similar to some versions of the Microcosmic Orbit - the circulation of chi in Chi Gong. Like Alternate Nostril Pranayama, it is great at the end of a warm up sequence. You may spontaneously go so deep into meditation that you will abandon the meditation technique you were planning to follow it with.

Do not strain in this breath. The only chance of injury in this exercise will occur if you strain the breath. The more relaxed you are, the more you will feel it in the spine. Relax into the spine during this exercise. Try some of the spine exercises in the Muscles and Soft Tissues section before you begin.

We will learn this in parts. When you are learning how to juggle five balls, it helps to learn how to juggle two balls first, then three, then five.

1. *The more relaxed and limber the spine, the easier it is to do this exercise. There are some great spine exercises in the Muscles and Soft Tissues section. Try this and remember to keep the legs relaxed during your Ujjayi practice.*

2. *Sit in sitting posture with back straight. Fix your Throat Lock Bandha by pulling your chin down and in toward the upper chest. Stack all your vertebra one on top of another, especially the upper vertebrae. The throat lock is 90% mental. It directs the breath up and down the spine so that the prana does not leak with an "airy sound". Your eyes are closed. However, if they were open, you would be staring straight ahead with nose pointing forward.*

3. *Place the bottom of your tongue to the roof of your mouth. The tip of your tongue is pointing toward the back of the mouth, as far back as it can go without strain. When you're completely relaxed, either in a few minutes or a few years, the tongue will enter the throat.*

4. *Stretch your forehead up so that the eyebrows are raised and there is pressure on the point between the eyebrows. There should be some "krinkle" in the forehead. Close your eyes and look into the spot between the eyebrows. Once this and the Throat Lock are in place, make sure that the jaw and tongue are relaxed.*

5. Empty your lungs completely with a slow exhale, then relax your belly for the next inhale.

6. With your Throat Lock, inhale completely through the nose, making the sound of distant ocean waves on the beach. It should be pretty loud and felt where your chest meets the back of the neck as well as the back of the palate where it meets the throat, but on top of the palate. At the same time, it should feel like it originates in your belly like a diaphragmatic breath. Your belly should not puff out. Your diaphragm will feel like it's massaging the spine in back of the naval while also massaging upward.

7. Hold for a couple seconds after the full inhale. Love your crown.

8. Exhale the same way you inhaled. Similar volume and force, feeling it in the same places, the same ocean wave sound, etc. Each inhale and exhale is probably about 10 seconds long.

9. Hold for a couple seconds and love your perineum. "See" the perineum with the third eye and crown.

10. Full inhale, hold, full exhale.

11. Keep practicing this before progressing further. You are doing this correctly if you stick a finger underneath your nostrils during the exhale and cannot feel air coming out of it. This means that you are exhaling carbonic acid instead of carbon dioxide. This is good. When you reach this point, try the next steps. If not, adjust your Throat Lock, clear any phlegm and relax into your spine.

12. *Note: The sound should be solid and consistent. If there are multiple sounds in the breath, especially "airy" sounds, it could be either phlegm or the throat lock need to be adjusted. Phlegm will definitely cause "leakage". You should probably stop, quickly clear your throat and swallow, then put your tongue back in place and continue.*

13. *Now, we're adding another element. When you inhale, follow the breath up from your perineum through the **back** of the spine. Your breath is going through each of your chakras and all the way up through the crown. Remember to hold and love your crown while basking in the stillness.*

14. *When you exhale, let the breath travel down the **front** of your spine, through the tongue via the pallet, through each chakra, all the way down to your perineum. **Do not force the breath up or down the spine**. It will feel like it's travelling at its own pace. You may see it as light or a feeling. It is possible that you will experience warm light rushing down the front of your body on the exhale. Remember to relax and watch the breath going up and down the spine.*

15. *One more element that you can add is the perineum bandha. When you begin the inhale, tighten and pull the perineum and anus back toward the spine. Guys will feel like they're holding back a pee. This bandha guides the energy up the spine more efficiently just as the tongue position guides the energy downward.*

16. *When you exhale, gradually release the perineum bandha.*

Some people will get a little winded at the end of an exhale. You can take a few shallow rapid breaths to get back on track. Then, empty the lungs, relax the belly and inhale again.

A good tip for you is, throughout the entire exercise, imagine yourself sitting in the top of your crown. You are watching the entire Ujjayi movie from there. When you note the stillness at the bottom of the breath, remember to watch it from the crown.

Asthmatics and insomniacs will love the Ujjayi Pranayama technique. If you are in relatively good health, you may extend the breath retention at the top and bottom while basking in the stillness. This is not recommended for some other health conditions. Insomnia is better treated without the breath retention.

The Taoists, in the Microcosmic Orbit, like to begin the circulation in the navel center and bring it down to the perineum. Then, they circulate the energy just as in this form of Ujjayi breathing. They will end the exercise in the navel center. The navel is good for storing chi, so maybe they have the right idea. Just a thought.

If you like this exercise, check out the Light and Sound Meditation for clues on going even further with Ujjayi.

Magic Portal Exercises

Bust out that list of your magic portals. Get your CD's, your spiritual writings, your favorite scriptures, maybe your favorite nature spot (you can visit it or imagine doing so), your favorite chants and prayers, fond memories and what not. Fit them all in an appropriate place in your program.

If you listen to a CD, you may do so during the entire warm-up. As for the meditation, you may wish to experiment with whether the music helps you or hinders you. Some work best in silence.

Perhaps you have a musical instrument that puts you into the meditative healing trance. If this is a sufficient warm-up for deep meditation, consider doing the muscle exercises first, then play your instrument and then meditate. You can also do a complete warm up routine, adding your instrument in the appropriate slot in the sequence. Be sure to experiment and find out through experience which methods work best.

Meditation Techniques

There are many types of meditation. However, there is only a small number of categories that one can categorize them in. Most meditation styles are repeats. They are the same techniques filtered through different cultures and languages.

The three factors - other than language and cultural symbols - that seem to vary in the multitude of techniques in a particular category are the object of focus, the warm up strategy and the methods of integrating the meditative awareness between practice sessions.

Everyone claims to have the best technique of them all. They are really arguing about who has the best symbols, who has the best warm up strategy or who has the best integration strategy. Experiment with the basic principles outlined in this book and you can turn any technique into "the best technique". Be sure to boast about it.

For these reasons, this section of the book is going to be a lot shorter than the warm ups section.

Remember that some of the warm up exercises can become meditations, too. If you slip into a meditative state, just flow like a river. Watch what's going on, including your thoughts, with detachment. You are watching form, energy and whatever you may perceive that transcends form and energy.

Body Scan Meditation

One of the simplest methods of meditation is the body scan. The body scan brings body awareness and concentration which spawns deep relaxation. With deep absorption, one slips into a state of meditation.

Be certain in this exercise that you are becoming increasingly and intimately aware of each body part that you are focusing on. You will notice subtle sensations that you are just not used to noticing. Get to know these sensations. Merge with them.

Body Scan

1. *Begin with a seated posture. Here, we will assume that you are in a chair with feet flat on the floor.*

2. *Close your eyes. Be conscious of your breath.*

3. *Watch the breath. If thoughts come up, let them be. You are the sky. They are the clouds. Gently bring attention back to the breath.*

4. *When your breathing naturally becomes diaphragmatically inspired, concentrate on the feet touching the floor. The bottoms of the feet are all that exist. If you get distracted, acknowledge the distraction and gently bring the attention back to the bottoms of the feet. Do this for at least a couple minutes.*

5. *Concentrate on your calves. Your calves are all that exist.*

6. *Do the same for your thighs.*

7. *Butt on chair is all that exists.*

8. *Genitals are all that exist.*

9. *Lower abdomen and back are all that exist.*

145

10. *The upper back and ribs are all that exist.*

11. *The hands are all that exist.*

12. *The upper arms and shoulders are all that exist.*

13. *Your neck is all that exists.*

14. *Your jaw is all that exists.*

15. *Your face is all that exists.*

16. *The back of your head is all that exists.*

17. *The top of your head and forehead are all that exists.*

18. *If you slip into a deep meditative state, stay with it without excitedly clinging to the experience or pushing away discomfort.*

Vipassana (Mindfulness)

Vipassana, as mentioned earlier in this book, is a Theravada Buddhist style of mindfulness meditation. Vipassana is the art of being fully present with yourself. With practice, you realize that you are not your thoughts. You are not your bodily sensations. You are not your cravings. You are not the false identity you created for yourself. You are the witness that is watching all the **rising and falling** without being touched by it. Such a witness is your true self.

With more practice, you realize that not only are you untouched by the **rising and falling**, but you are also an intimate part of it. You are realizing Shiva, then Shakti.

As you learn to watch your own mind, you also learn which programs your mental computer is running on. Instead of identifying with your programs, you are seeing that they are just programs. It is much easier to dissolve "bad" programs and create "good" programs with such awareness. It is also much easier to not take offense when someone challenges your programs. They are not you and you know it.

Some people find it really hard to sit with themselves for an hour or two in one sitting. In such a case, you can begin by sitting for 15 minutes at a time and taking breaks between them. You may just chill out or you can practice some warm up exercises during these intermissions.

Much of this section will be repeat information.

In Vipassana, you begin by watching the natural flow of your breath. As you become mindful of the breath, it will gradually deepen and become guided by the diaphragm.

We learned two points of focus during Vipassana breathing; the feeling in the nostrils and the navel. When you concentrate on the feeling in the nostrils, you do not mentally follow the breath in and out. You are concentrating only on the feeling in the nostrils. If you need more specific information, try concentrating just below the nostrils and above the upper lip. This is where you'll feel the breath. Otherwise, you can focus on the feeling of "coolness" just inside the nostrils. Concentration on the nostril area develops concentration and prevents drowsiness. To dispel distracting thought, you can concentrate on the navel center (a couple inches below the navel and a couple inches in) instead while breathing through the nose.

The third method of breathing is the author's favorite. In this method, you are following the "river of breath". The breath is like a river entering and leaving your body. Follow the river without being attached to how it flows. After a while, you will feel like you are breathing with your skin instead of your lungs, nose and trachea. You may feel the breath as consciousness inflating various parts of your body, gradually clearing tension and bringing balance to the body. As you develop this awareness, you establish a better connection with your environment in daily life. Your stream of consciousness will flow, with each breath, to wherever it is needed most.

For the exercise, we will assume that you are focusing on the nostril area.

1. *Assume a seated posture, including the sensory awareness training. Relax in your preferred manner.*

2. *If you can keep your eyes 9/10 shut, do so. Otherwise, close your eyes.*

3. *Place your tongue on your palate, pointing it back toward the throat as far back as is comfortable. Tuck in your chin like in the throat bandha and stack your vertebrae. Relax the tongue, eyes and jaw.*

4. *Focus on the breath as it enters your nostrils. Do not follow the breath in and out. Just be present with the feeling where your nostrils meet the area above your lips or the feeling of coolness in the nostrils. Do not control the breath. Relax into the breath and be the breath. The inhale and exhale should be even in length and quality.*

5. *If your mind wanders, let your thoughts be. You are the sky. They are the clouds. Note that you are thinking without pushing away the thoughts.*

6. *Gently bring the mind back to the breath. Develop a good sense of concentration. The breath will gradually deepen and be guided by the diaphragm.*

7. *Your brain is like a spoiled child. It will try to trick you into giving up. You may experience enticing thoughts or even itching. Be present with these thoughts and sensations, noting that they are happening. Gently bring your attention back to the breath. The key to Vipassana is perseverance.*

8. *You may experience "stuck" energy loosening up. This may reveal emotions you did not know you had, even murder. Be present with everything and let the ice melt. That is the only way to let it go. Remember that the body is the key to the subconscious mind. Stuff will bubble up to the surface. It is the first step to greater joy and peace in the long run.*

Equanimity is what we are gradually developing through Vipassana Meditation. With practice, less of the things of this world will bother you as you become more in touch with the mandates of your inner teacher.

There is a lot of literature on Vipassana Meditation in books, on the internet and elsewhere. In a search engine, you may type in the keywords Vipassana Meditation, Mindfulness Meditation or Insight Meditation for more information on this practice. They all mean the same thing.

Breath Counting

Breath counting is a great way to develop concentration. With practice, you will develop a spontaneous "pause" at the top

149

and bottom of each breath. Total inner stillness and deep knowledge of the absolute are revealed in these pauses.

The following exercise will look somewhat similar to Vipassana, but simpler. The simplicity does not make it less valuable. It is all a matter of what you connect with most.

Breath Counting Meditation

1. *Begin in a seated posture. Perform the whole seated posture exercise, including the sensory orientation training and the tongue position.*

2. *Tuck in your chin toward the upper chest while "stacking" your vertebrae one on top of another. Your nose points forward. This is somewhat similar to the Throat Lock Bandha in Ujjayi Pranayama.*

3. *Close your eyes or use the 9/10 method. Breathe through the nose. Be mindful of the breath until it naturally deepens and becomes diaphragmatic.*

4. *Count each inhale as one breath. If your mind wanders, let your thoughts move through you like clouds in the sky. Don't push them away. Gently guide your attention back to the breath.*

5. *Remember that the inhale and exhale should be even and very similar in length and quality.*

6. *You want to count at least 100 inhales without losing count. If you lose count, start over.*

7. *With practice, you will become more aware of the space between inhales and exhales. These are moments of*

great stillness. If you are relaxed, you may spontaneously pause at the top and bottom of each breath. The pauses are just as important as the breathing. Get to know these pauses.

One trick which just might help you still your thoughts before breath counting (other than the warm-up routine) is the practice of being present with the left side of your body. Start with your left hand. Just be present with your left hand, then your left arm, then your left leg, etc. The right side of your brain will temporarily take over the show and calm your thoughts.

Presence Meditation

Presence meditation cultivates the ability to be present with both yourself and the external environment. You will gradually develop consciousness of the infinite. Your third eye will gradually develop toward its full potential. You may, with lots of practice, develop 360° vision or "omnidirectional awareness".

The meditation comes in when you slip into a deep sense of presence without clinging to anything or pushing it away.

Presence Meditation

1. *Perform the complete sitting posture exercise, including the sensory orientation training. Your tongue should be on your palate. You are breathing through your nose.*
2. *Be conscious of your whole environment while feeling inside your body.*
3. *You are breathing through the nose, being present with yourself and your environment.*
4. *During an exhale, close your eyes and project consciousness from your third eye infinitely in all directions. Realize that space continues infinitely in*

every direction and that you have the ability to be
conscious of and present with it.

5. *Try to feel the environment. Remind yourself of the One
Consciousness in all things.*
6. *Try to see everything in the immediate environment
with your inner eye. This ability will increase over time.*

Inner Light and Sound Meditation

But the holy stream of Sound, the Holy Stream of
Life (life force, vibration),
and the Holy Stream of Light, these were never
born, and can never die.
Enter the Holy Streams, even that Life, that
Light, and that Sound which
gave you birth; that you may reach the kingdom of
the Heavenly Father and become
one with him, even as the river empties into the
far distant sea.

-**Jesus**, Essene Gospel of Peace, from Aramaic

The proper practice of the Inner Light and Sound
Meditation has one prerequisite. You must already be conscious of
the inner light and sound. Close your eyes. What do you see in your
forehead? Do you see darkness? Do you see tiny, dynamic speckles
of light? A vibration of some kind? If you see the speckles or a
dynamic vibration, you may be ready for light and sound
meditation. Otherwise, you can follow the steps below while
turning it into a visualization exercise. In other words, just imagine
the light in the body.

What do you hear when everything is totally silent and
still? Do you hear frequencies or subtle tones? Perhaps a subtle
ocean type sound? If so, you may be in touch with the inner sound.
Otherwise, you will be when relaxation increases.

Scientists may explain the inner light and sound as a result of the electrical system of the body. This may be true. However, we are more interested in practical applications rather than theory. Meditating on the light and sound leads to deep perception of the primordial om vibration in all things which, in turn, leads to consciousness of the one spirit in all things. Your intuition will also increase.

Inner Light and Sound Meditation

1. *Begin with the entire seated posture exercise with your tongue on the palette. Close your eyes. Breathe through the nose.*

2. *Notice the inner light in your forehead and the inner sound in your head. This light and sound exists everywhere in the universe. However, just be present with it in your head. Relax into the light and sound and merge with it.*

3. *Be present with the light and sound in your face.*

4. *Be present with the light and sound in your jaw.*

5. *Be present with the light and sound in the back of your head.*

6. *Be present with the light and sound on the top of your head. If you perceive it above your crown, be present with that, too.*

7. *Proceed with the neck, upper chest and upper back, abdomen and lower back, genital area, thighs, calves, ankles and feet, then the tips of the toes.*

8. The light and sound may change form as you remain present with it for a while and your perception of it deepens.

9. Empty your lungs, relax your belly and inhale completely. Lean forward with your crown pointing straight ahead. Your back is as straight as possible with hands clasped behind it, resting near your tailbone. Exhale. Realize the light and sound in your head, especially in the back of your head which is facing up at the moment. Be present with it and relax into it.

10. Twist the spine and move your upper body to the left so that your right shoulder is pointing straight up and the right side of your head is pointing up. Be present with the light and sound in your head, especially the right side of your head.

11. Repeat the light and sound saturation of step 9. The back of your head is facing up.

12. Twist to the right so that your left shoulder is pointing straight up and the left side of your head is facing up. Be present with the light and sound in your head, especially the left side of your head.

13. Repeat the light and sound saturation of step 9 again.

14. Inhale completely through nose with an Ujjayi breath.

15. Hold breath while becoming vertical again in the seated posture.

16. Exhale completely through nose with an Ujjayi breath.

17. *Continue to be present with the light and sound and notice any vibration in the body.*

18. *Breathe normally and realize that the light and sound is in all things. You are connected to everything in the universe.*

19. *Practice Ujjayi Breathing technique to circulate the light and sound through the body and spine. Be conscious as it penetrates and purifies each energy center. At the top of the breath, be present with the light and sound in the crown and beyond it. At the bottom of the breath, be present with the light and sound in the perineum. Do this for a while.*

20. *When you are ready, try this. At the top of one breath, after the pause, project the light and sound from the crown, infinitely in all directions, into the whole universe. Be present with the whole universe.*

21. *You are in a space beyond light and sound, beyond breath. Be present with the one consciousness in all things. Embrace the All. The light and sound within you merges with the light and sound of the whole universe.*

22. *Sit in meditation for a while and be present, relaxing into the All.*

Third Eye Meditations

Third eye meditations increase intuition and promote stillness of mind. Physical warm-ups and Ujjayi Pranayama are recommend before performing these techniques. It may also be to your benefit if you follow a third eye meditation with an inner smile and a round of "Gather Chi into your Navel Tan Tien". These grounding and balancing exercises will provide some protection against unwanted side effects associated with focusing exclusively on the third eye.

Simple Third Eye Meditation

1. *Perform the entire sitting posture exercise, including the tongue position.*

2. *Breathe through the nose and close your eyes.*

3. *Pull your eyes about 25 degrees upward and look into the point between the eyebrows. You will know it when you hit the right spot. It will feel "just right" with a gentle strain on the eyes. Your eyes will be calm, relaxed and motionless.*

4. *Be present with your third eye and the breath. Relax into it.*

5. *As you develop this state of awareness, you will be more present with your thoughts. Vipassana type qualities will begin to develop automatically.*

Om Meditation

1. *Repeat the Simple Third Eye Meditation exercise.*

2. *On the inhale, mentally repeat "OOOOOOOOOO" as in "om".*

3. *Pause. Enjoy the stillness.*

4. *Exhale while mentally repeating "MMMMMMMM". Let the "O" and the "M" be of even length.*

5. *A variation on this is to say "om" out loud on the exhale with the "O" equal in length as the "M". Pause at the top and bottom of each breath. Near the end of your practice, let the om gradually become quieter.*

6. *You can also mentally repeat the entire om on the inhale and om on the exhale, but not during the pauses.*

7. *In any case, become increasingly present with the subtle vibrations of "om".*

Cathartic Meditation

The cathartic approach to meditation was probably popularized, but not invented by, Osho. Osho was the king of spontaneity meditations involving dancing, whirling and the like. An internet search for Meditations of Osho will bring up a lot of results.

A dynamic "warm-up" is built into this exercise. Make sure that you are physically healthy for this one. Be conscious of your environment, too, so that you don't get hurt.

Cathartic Meditation

1. *Begin in any position. Breathe full inhales and exhales through the nose. The breathing is somewhat fast and strong. Move your body in any way that you wish during the breathing stage. Do this stage for 5 or 10 minutes.*

2. *Go crazy! Crank up some wild music and flail around, dancing spontaneously or beating up a Teddy Bear. If you feel aggression, let it out, but safely. Perform this stage for up to 20 minutes.*

3. *Sit in a seated posture. Breathe through the nose and enjoy the silence. Any meditation technique works well for this.*

Binaural Beats

You may have seen ads that say "instantly meditate like a master" or "instant deep meditation". These ads are usually for audio products that "entrain" your brainwaves to vibrate at lower frequencies.

Just in case you are unfamiliar with the brainwave frequency ranges, we'll have a brief synopsis.

Beta – 12-24 cycles per second - normal waking activity

Alpha – 8-12 cycles per second - deep relaxation, watching a sunset

Theta – 4-8 cycles per second - dreaming, waking dreams, very deep meditation

Delta – 0.5-4 cycles per second - deep dreamless sleep - very very very deep meditation

Epsilon – less than 0.5 cycles per second

Gamma – 24-70 cycles per second and usually around 40 - this one's more complicated

Binaural beats are audio products that are used with stereo headphones. An audio impulse is played inaudibly in each ear. You cannot hear the sounds. They are covered with soft music or nature sounds. The difference in the frequencies of these impulses is the same frequency that your brainwaves will be vibrating at. For example, one tone is 200Hz and another is 195Hz. This will entrain your brainwaves to vibrate at 5Hz, a Theta wave.

Furthermore, suppose one tone is 100Hz and the other is 95Hz. You will still be in a Theta state. However, the effect on your brainwaves and physiology will have more impact. As a result, some companies offer programs with graduated courses of Delta wave entrainment. You use one "level" for one hour per day and then you "graduate" to the next four months later when your brain get used to the changes.

Binaural beats are an excellent part of any healthy routine. However, don't believe the hype about them being the alternative to spiritual and stress reduction practice. Binaural beats will do many things quickly that meditation may not do as quickly, such as rapidly toning up the entire glandular system and awakening chakras. However, meditation practice will give you all these benefits plus concentration, peaceful balance, discipline and a well trained heart and mind. These are things that binaural beats cannot offer.

Therefore, binaural beats are a great COMPLEMENT to meditation practice, but not an alternative.

BB will definitely enhance Vipassana and other mindfulness practices. Some techniques that depend on particular brainwave progressions may clash with it. The BB may start with a Beta state and gradually plunge into Delta. This may interfere with what your particular technique is trying to accomplish. Whatever the case, BB is definitely worth a try... just don't believe the instant Zen master hype.

Some of the originators of binaural technology charge close to $1,000 bucks for the complete graduated Delta meditation program. However, there are cheaper alternatives.

Progressive Relaxation

Progressive Relaxation is a method for systematically inducing relaxation in the body while retaining an alert mind. Progressive Relaxation is possible through the inner smile and self hypnosis. However, our example exercise will demonstrate the clench and release approach.

This is a popular yogic method of Progressive Relaxation using the "Clench and Release" method in a systematic way.

Progressive "Clench and Release" Relaxation

1. *You may sit in seated posture or lie on your back with arms to the sides. Do not do this in a space that you mentally associate with sleep.*

2. *Close your eyes and breathe through the nose during this exercise.*

3. *Clench your feet and toes. Release and feel the difference in your feet and toes. Mentally repeat an "anchor phrase" such as "relax and release". Breathe into the feet and allow them to relax.*

4. *Go all the way up the body – anywhere you can clench and release. Remember your anchor phrase.*

5. *After getting the whole body, breathe deeply through the nose and feel the sensations in the entire body. If you find any more tension, clench and release the area and use the anchor phrase.*

6. *When you slip into a state of meditation, just flow with it, watching the whole show, including your thoughts. Be open and spacious.*

7. *After a lot of practice, your anchor phrase will become very powerful in itself.*

For other exercises, you may type "free guided meditation" in a search engine. Many of them are progressive relaxation techniques. Most of them are just people with hypnotic voices guiding you into relaxation.

Mantra and Prayer Meditations

Mantra meditation is similar to chant, but it deals with a particular word or short phrase. Sometimes the word has meaning. Sometimes it is a nonsense word with particular vibrational qualities.

Mantra Meditation

1. *Pick a word such as "peace".*

2. *Remember all the steps for effective chanting in the "Exercises for the Emotions" section. When you inhale, do so through the nose, being aware of your breath or silently aware of the mantra.*

3. *You can recite the word or sing it to any tune you wish. Keep repeating it. Make the word "peace" (for example) long or short, whichever works better. Longer syllables are usually more conducive for meditation.*

4. *Close your eyes.*

5. *Pay particular attention to the vibrations of the word in the mind and body.*

6. *Let the vibrations work through any and all tension in the body.*

7. *If any distracting thoughts come up, let them do their thing. Then, gently bring your attention back to the mantra.*

8. *Slowly fade the word until you are uttering it silently. If you have been reciting it silently all along, ignore this step.*

9. *If you slip into meditation, become the loving observer of the sensations in your body, your thoughts and whatever you perceive that is beyond body, thoughts and energy.*

A prayer meditation is similar to a mantra meditation. Recite your favorite prayer over and over again while following the steps above. An example is "Lord, make me an instrument of your peace" on the exhale. Next exhale: "Where there is hatred, let me so love", etc.

Sensual Meditation

Sensual Meditation was "discovered" by the Raelian movement which began in 1974. Sensual Meditation is much more than a technique that will be described here. It is a whole system of detached sensory awareness and the shedding of taboos.

Sensual Meditation

1. *Perform the Vipassana technique.*

162

2. *Open your eyes half way. Keep doing Vipassana, but add the following elements:*

3. *Notice what you see. Watch impartially, just as you are watching your thoughts and breath. Notice what you hear. Notice what you smell. Notice what you feel. Notice what you taste.*

Walking Meditation

Walking meditation is like Vipassana in motion.

Walking Meditation

1. *Stand in a spacious room or outdoors. Clasp your hands behind your back. Eyes are defocused and turned inward. You are looking outward and inward at the same time, feeling inside the body.*

2. *You are going to be walking in a straight line.*

3. *Place all your weight on your left foot. Lift the right foot.*

4. *Bring the right foot forward. Place the heel of the right foot on the floor.*

5. *Gradually apply more weight onto your right heel and less on your left foot. Bring your right "ball of foot" to the floor as you shift the weight on your left to the ball of the left foot.*

6. *Bring your right toes to the floor so that your right foot is flat on the floor.*

7. *Lift the heel of your left foot.*

163

8. *Shift the weight of the right foot to the toes while lifting the right heal. At the same time, take all weight off the left foot.*

9. *Lift the left foot and slowly bring it forward, placing the left heel on the ground. At the same time, begin taking weight off the right foot.*

10. *Touch the ball of the left foot to the floor, then the toes. As the toes touch the floor, lift the heel of the right foot. Shift all the weight to the left foot.*

11. *Bring the right foot forward, touching the heel to the floor.*

12. *If you're confused, remember heel-ball-toe-heel-ball-toe... You are gradually shifting the weight burden from one foot to the other while noting when heel, ball and toe touch the floor.*

13. *When you are about to hit a wall, turn around with a smooth "pivot".*

14. *Always be mindful of the feeling of heal-ball-toe touching the floor as well as the shifting of body weight. Be mindful of the breath. If thoughts occur, be mindful of them as clouds in the sky.*

Concept Meditation

Concept Meditation is the focusing on a spiritual concept such as "spaciousness", "infinity", "gratitude", a pyramid, God or a spiritual figure. If your mind wanders from this concept, you allow your thoughts to be and then you gently bring your mind back to the concept. You will gradually become aware of the reality behind the concept that you are focusing on. Enjoy infinity when you find it.

The following exercise is a rather complex form of Concept Meditation.

Who Am I? Meditation

The Who Am I Meditation was popularized by Ramana Maharshi. The goal is to realize that you are pure Spirit.

1. *Assume the meditation posture of your choice. Relax using your preferred method.*

2. *Concentrate on the question, "Who Am I?" Thoughts will come up. Know that none of these thoughts describe who you are. Ok. You're a mailman. No, you're not. That's not who you truly are. The important thing here is who you are not rather than who you think you are.*

3. *If you're still really sure, after doing this for a while, that you still know who you are, then pick up a copy of The Book by Alan Watts and try this exercise again.*

Grounding Meditation into Everyday Life

We have learned how to use warm ups to tune ourselves for deep meditation. We have also learned the five minute intertwine or "interweaving", "bathing" and "projecting" and mindful eating as well as the initial stages of integration after formal meditation practice.

Now comes the tricky part: Integrating this "tuned in" awareness into everyday activities.

Let's begin by observing a cat after a catnap. What does the cat do? It stretches. Some of us do this, too. Perhaps we all should follow this example. This is the first step to a great day. If there is no rush, then start your intertwine first thing in the morning.

In meditation we learn to watch our own minds as an impartial observer. Our subconscious programs and associated thoughts run on autopilot throughout the day. The more we change these programs, the more we realize that they are not who we really are. Before this realization occurs, we think that we are these thoughts.

How do we make sure that our programs do not have power over us?

Mindfulness.

We have learned what brings mindfulness. Impartially watching our thoughts, breathing and body awareness, becoming the observer. Therefore, let us carry this awareness throughout the day. The intertwine will greatly help us to break through the hypnotic state. It will create a feeling of "opening" followed by a greater awareness of the programs we are running on.

A good trick to incorporate into your intertwine is to observe yourself in the 1st, 2nd and 3rd person. Look through another's eyes. Jump out of your body and look at yourself, your situation and your thoughts and feelings from multiple camera angles. Try this whenever you feel agitated or upset.

Even more important than the intertwine is remembering to breathe consciously, even when you're busy. If you have troubles coordinating this with driving a car, then please choose safety first. However, we can learn to integrate conscious breathing into every activity. You may become a better driver.

Another method of integration is the art of conscious relationships. Remember the sensory orientation exercises in the Posture section? This will help us to see ourselves in other people, events and things. Learn how to integrate this awareness into your daily interactions if you haven't already. If you already have, then learn how to do it more deeply and solidly. It's a process and not a goal.

Don't let any interaction interrupt your smooth pattern of breath. Breath is awareness and feeling. When we don't want to feel something, we tend to shut down the breath. Do not fall for this trick. If you begin to fall for it, then try inhaling through your mouth and out your nose until you can come back into smooth nasal breathing.

Assume everyone is God. Spirit may be acting or speaking through a person to teach us.

For more information on integrating meditation into interpersonal relationships, please read the Appendix.

What gifts have the North American indigenous tribes given us? There is one that comes to mind, and that is reverence. When building and preparing for sweatlodge ceremonies, the

Lakota give thanks to every natural material that is used in the process from construction to the ceremony itself. Reverence connects you with the essence within all things. Try this with people, too, including your teachers who have wronged in the eyes of your belief structure.

Always remember the call to service. We are all called to service in a unique way. Pay attention and listen to that call.

Your feet hit the ground many times when you walk. Are you aware of it? Let it become a meditation. Try allowing your movements to originate from your core. Start with your center of gravity. Centered movement contributes to a centered mind. Walk to the rhythm of a chant. Go for a walk and listen to nature.

When you become more mindful in everyday life, "stuff" will come up. We had this talk in the Detoxification section. This can be likened to thawing ice. Stuck energy loosens.

When you begin cleaning a floor, you will agitate a lot of dirt. Your house will look dirtier in the beginning until the sweeping and scrubbing is finished. Just like the broom or the mop, mindfulness both agitates and clears debris.

Are you feeling agitated? Hyperactive? You have control over a jackhammer when your body is vibrating with it. Otherwise, it will throw you around. Use the intertwine to synchronize your consciousness with this energy. You will harmonize with it. This is the first step to relaxing agitated states of mind. If you have troubles relaxing after synchronizing, then perhaps you need such a state of mind for an important task. Otherwise, relax into it rather than away from it.

Remember the jackhammer analogy while reading the appendix on conflict resolution.

There is a bumper sticker which instructs us to "Expect Miracles". This does not mean that we must always expect water being turned into wine. Mini-miracles happen every day. The more "in the flow" we are, the more conscious we are of these miracles. Synchronicities are those meaningful coincidences that nudge us along on our path. We may think of a long lost person and then see them afterward. We may ask the universe a question and then witness a book which provides the answer falling off a high shelf. There does not seem to be a clear cause and effect between these events, or at least we can't trace them. A process is occurring that is larger than our intellects.

To such people, I say that God is everywhere, not in a particular form, but as an omnipresent awareness or power. God is consciousness itself, and by concentrated, sincere prayer, you are tuning your mental radio to receive that power. If I say there is nice music in this room, some of you may disagree and say, "We don't hear any music. How can you say that there is music in the room?" To you, I say get a radio, tune it properly, and you will hear the music.

-Swami Satchidananda

Synchronicities can occur as an answer to a supplicating prayer or they can be "clues" to our next stage of the unfolding of consciousness. Expect them and pay attention to their messages. Feel their messages within. If you aren't aware of such coincidences, keep on the path of meditation and "tune your mental radio".

The main thing to remember in our integration process is that, in each moment, we have a choice of what to do with our bodies and minds. The word "nourishment" comes to mind. We must "consume" what is nourishing and activate our emotional/spiritual digestive system for optimum health.

We can be as creative with the integration process as we wish. Remember that the effects of positive habits are cumulative like the river carving the Grand Canyon.

Appendix

Resolving Conflict with Our Whole Being

A Practical Guide to Everyday Peace

By Tom Von Deck

I Love Trademarks

Note: This is a polished transcript of a free class that the author taught on 04/11/06.

The name of this class, or workshop or whatever you wish to call it is "A Jedi Training Experience in Psychic Self Defense". We can call it many things such as: Processing the present moment in interpersonal relations, finding center in challenging situations, neutralization of disharmonic elements in our interpersonal environment, harmonizing with conflict, the art of peace, which was a book written by the founder of Aikido, the art of battle or the art of presence. We can give it a one word name such as love or harmony.

There are many names we can give it. There are many ways to describe it. We can approach it from a psychological perspective, in terms of energy, or a spiritual level, or physical. This is because it is a holistic process. We're working on all levels.

Models are never true. They only serve a functional purpose. In this case, the purpose is to give the intellect something to grab onto so that we can consciously put these principles into practice. True understanding comes through experiencing something with the entire being. The intellect will never understand this stuff because it is only a fragment.

We all know this stuff already. I'm not here to teach anything. My job is simply to facilitate the triggering of an internal process. Models are never true. I really don't believe a word that I'm saying right now.

The way in which it will all be presented, the structure, will resemble the structure of battle. However, it's the flipside to battle. It is that which increases communion, dissolving polarization and separation, rather than that which reinforces separation.

Just to set the stage a bit, this pair of hair clippers here. What is it? In relation to our senses and minds, some may see it as a solid object with particular qualities. Some may see it as a pattern of condensed light. If we use our intellects, we can break it down into atoms and so on. Between the nucleus of the atom and the electrons is almost entirely empty space. Between the atoms, same thing, empty space. Every solid object is mainly empty space. We can further divide the nucleus into subatomic particles, and those into quarks. Past that level, all you get is tiny vibrations of light.

Is there a reality to what we perceive as the clippers? Only in relation to our senses and our minds. Therefore, the most honest thing I can say about this pair of clippers is that it's simply an experience inside of myself.

Would anyone like to shave my head? (A volunteer emerges).

Whenever I treat everything this way, softening the gaze inward, I find that my intuitions and hunches about things are much more correct. I'm not stumbling in darkness as much. This is only the first step, however.

Let's say that over the next ten years, as the inward gaze softens and deepens, I experience a series of transformations of consciousness. Through softening, experience deepens. Let's say that in ten years, I have a partner. I look into her eyes and see nothing but the one Lover behind all lovers. Then, I remember partners past and see nothing but the same Woman with the same purpose manifesting Herself through various forms. The direction of soul perception is always in the direction of oneness – oneness and wholeness. All events lead us in this direction if we treat the events correctly, from our core, seeing the common purpose of everything. There will be more on this later.

As the inward gaze relaxes and deepens then, more and more, our two external eyes merge into one. Then we're seeing more and more with the eye between the eyes. The external eyes see the tension between opposites, the polarization, the duality – the two. The spiritual eye sees only the one. So, as the inward gaze softens, everything gradually becomes one thing. The fragments fall away. It's all one process.

Cultivating inner awareness is just as important as cultivating the heart. By cultivating, I mean relaxing and allowing a deeper and deeper experience. They both lead to compassion – seeing self in others, seeing others in self, seeing the One in all. From the New Testament: "If thine eye be single, thy whole body shall be full of light."

Now, let's look at the form of this class, workshop, whatever we wish to call it. With an external awareness, there is a supposed expert on the subject. Then there is the peanut gallery. Words and ideas come from me, travel through the air somehow, and are then processed by your minds. Each of us has a world view, a set of assumptions about how things work. My world view expresses itself and interacts with yours to confirm, add to or refute what you already hold.

Well, we know that all models are false. There's nothing I can say and nothing you can think which measures up to the great, great vastness of absolute truth anyway. So, let's scrap this whole model. We're all reflections inside of each other. We're all experiences. The thoughts that come up throughout this session rise and fall like waves. All the people in the room - It's a sea of experience. Attraction and repulsion – clinging to comfort and pushing away discomfort. It's all just energy – just experience. Sensations in the body – like clouds in the sky. Let's allow it to move through us. Relax. Breathe.

I was going to facilitate a guided meditation so that we can embody this more fully, but I'll be yapping for long time and it may be better to make room for discussion.

Let's all put our pointer fingers just below the navel. The middle finger just below that touching the pointer finger. Then the ring finger touching the middle. Then the pinky. Breathing from center begins with the abdomen. We want to push out all four fingers with equal pressure on the inhale. The diaphragm is massaging above, below, forward and backward at the same time like a balloon. Through the nose, let's breathe. They teach this stuff right there at the yoga studio across the parking lot. It's centered breathing.

Now, the full breath. It starts with a partial abdominal breath. Then we partially fill the lower chest, then the middle chest, and then the upper chest, raising our shoulders a little bit. Then, on the exhale, the exact reverse. It's more involved than that, but with practice it becomes more natural anyway. We chopped this up into four parts. However, as we practice and our experience of it deepens, relaxing into the process, then the fragments fall away. It's all one motion.

So... the Jedi Knights, Shambhala warriors, spiritual warriors, fighting monks – what's it all about? We're only going to touch one aspect of this, but this one aspect touches upon everything else, too. As mentioned earlier, the intellect is never going to understand this stuff. True understanding comes only with practice – always softening, always deepening. To quote Ammachi, "God is pure experience."

We will chop all this into parts: Recognizing Divine Intent or "Common Purpose" (wholeness) in conflict, breath, grounding, matching the energy, processing feeling in body, giving up resentment, facing ourselves, etc. These parts are untrue. They serve a functional purpose, as mentioned earlier. The magic glue that binds it back together is practice. It all moves from spirit into form so that our intellects can grab onto something and, through practice, bring it back to spirit – back to pure experience. When we put it into practice, the fragments fall away. It's all one process. Reality is seemless.

Has anyone studied Tai Chi? Push Hands? (The Barber explained some of the principles, on request, of Push Hands, in terms of grounding, keeping centered, connecting with the Earth as well as the subtle energy circuit between both participants and the Earth, while cutting hair. The barber was cutting hair, that is.)

Some forms of push hands are more competitive than others. In some schools, both opponents are rocking back and forth, attempting to exploit a weakness in the other, using the other person's energy to throw them off-balance. Some instructors call it "Sensing Hands", and prefer a model of healing partners rather than opponents. When the process touches upon a little pocket of tension, a non-integrated weakness in the bodymind, then there's a stop in the flow. That person is then given a chance to breathe into that weakness and soften it, allowing that pocket of tension to integrate itself into the whole. Every conflict can be transformed in this way.

In some martial arts tournaments, both opponents bow to each other before whooping ass. This is only an empty shell of a much deeper process. It's like holding a rosary in your hand and mechanically uttering "Hail Mary full of grace the Lord is with thou blessed art thou..." over and over again. The rosary can be a great practice. The magic fuel that powers it is LSD – Love, Surrender, Devotion – ever softening, ever deepening.

Everyone is both personality and soul. The personality is the self of identity - that which clings and claims a piece of the All for itself. The All is split into two. It's the self of duality. Duality leads to tension in the bodymind. It's a fierce polarization between opposite poles. When there's a little pocket of tension in the bodymind, there's separation, right? It's not integrated into the whole. That pocket of tension vibrates out into the external in the form of interpersonal polarization and separation. This creates dynamics between people.

Whenever someone is attacking us in some way, they are carrying a little pocket of tension within themselves. They are latching onto a little pocket of tension within us by polarity. It's often a common weakness or a similar but opposite weakness. There's something within both parties that is not integrated into wholeness. In a relationship, there is something that is preventing communion. There is an unmet need that needs to be discovered.

Both parties are always seeking wholeness. This is always the intent of the soul – The Divine Intent. Remembering the Divine Intent and Common Purpose (wholeness) is the first step to approaching conflict from a point of centeredness and spaciousness. Spaciousness is the goal - the final frontier. No one can mess with space. There's nothing to grab onto when you're fighting space.

Let's say that someone is attacking you and they're calling you on a weakness. Even if their perception of your weakness is wrong, it doesn't matter. No opinion is true. However, on some level, they are absolutely correct. To find the true weakness that they are poking at, we must feel it within our own body. Finding our own weakness is the gateway to spaciousness. Then, our job is to soften it. When we do this, the antagonist is forced, though a mirror effect, to confront their own corresponding weakness. This is called "The knockout punch". We must hold space for the person, allowing them to process the experience.

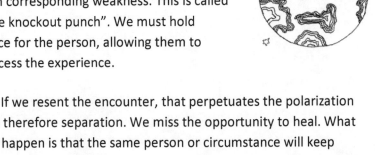

If we resent the encounter, that perpetuates the polarization and therefore separation. We miss the opportunity to heal. What will happen is that the same person or circumstance will keep reappearing, either in the same form or in a different form, until we soften that weakness, allowing it to integrate.

In the Beatitudes, Yehoshua (Jesus) said, "Blessed are those who soften what is rigid, for they shall receive strength and sustenance from nature, or the Earth, or the subtle forces of creation." There are many ways to translate it from the Aramaic.

If we welcome the blessing and soften what is rigid within ourselves, then we receive strength and sustenance and natural support. If we don't soften what is rigid, then nature will do it for us. We must bow to the other soul and sincerely thank them for helping us to find where we're not whole. Whatever we truly bow to bows back to us. It has no choice.

I worked at a bunch of gas stations. Gas stations are great practice for all this stuff. I used to make it a practice to end each shift with more energy than when I started. After a while, it was very consistent, no matter how many crabby customers came in. It involved a lot of chanting, too – that always helped to create that healing trance.

One time, in the middle of the night, this gangbanger type of guy walked in. The wireless phone was out of juice. The phone in the wall had a faulty connection, so making a call was impossible. The payphone was also broken.

He wanted to use the phone. When he found out that he couldn't, he cussed me out very fiercely.

I silently built up inner strength, starting with the breath. I felt the feet on ground, connecting with the biomagnetism of the earth, and then the sky. I followed the lines of energy to my own weakness in my own bodymind. From this centered position, I was able to see the root of the conflict rather than the periphery. It was clear that both of our corresponding defense mechanisms were having a dance. His came from the fear of getting the short end of the stick, or something like that, and mine was to shut down feeling, probably to avoid conflict.

There was a common weakness, similar but opposite. Two opposite poles – one passive, one aggressive.

I allowed him to work on my weakness so that I could begin to match his energy. Then, it became possible to mirror his negativity back to him – not in an imbalanced way, with a desire to hurt or to make him wrong, but in a way that came from my center. When his energy was mirrored back to him, it took on the form, not of aggression, but assertiveness. This further helped me to clear my weakness. The whole time, I allowed all the sensation of the experience to flow through my bodymind like clouds through the sky.

At some point, he walked toward the door. Normally, it is better to let them do that. This time, however, I felt that there was unfinished business, and besides, I felt 100% protection. So, I got the last word in. He froze, turned around in full rage, walked toward me, and stared me down with the look of death.

I allowed it to burn though my weakness – the magic portal – while practicing centeredness. I'm not sure what happened after that, whether he asked for something or not, but I thought the situation was a pretty cool experience. I offered him a drink.

Immediately, his heart opened up to the point of choking back tears. All he could say was "You a good person. You a good person." When we face ourselves, the other is forced to do the same. When we truly bow to someone, they have no choice but to bow back.

Afterward, we went outside for a smoke. He told me that, at one point, he thought I was about to take out a gun and shoot him.

It was not the external act of offering him something which caused this. It was the entire process, both internal and external. There is no separation between the internal and the external. This illusion offers nothing but a lot of boring churches and centers of worship. We're taught from the beginning that whatever goes on within doesn't matter. Only the outer expression matters. This leads to error, because the outer action is dead. There's no life in it unless it originates from within.

If we practice all these principles, experiencing the process on deeper and deeper levels, then whatever anyone tries to do to us, they end up doing it to themselves. This is called "The Droopy effect" – an activation of the "Spirit Mist Mirror", to borrow a term from my former roommate – a martial arts and meditation teacher. When we fully process the moment in the reality of the moment, the karmic reaction becomes an instant process. The attacker is, metaphorically, fighting with a giant slingshot. They try to headbutt the slingshot, but it absorbs all the energy of the blow. Then, what happens?

Even in extreme situations, following these principles works. From centeredness, you're in a much better position to know whether to fight or run and how to fight or run. You can know when to hold 'em, know when to fold 'em, know when to walk away, know when to run. Infinite possibilities for creation are present. That's the nature of spaciousness.

Let's break it down.

Breath and Grounding

When we restrict breath, we restrict feeling, and vice versa. Whenever we feel grounded and connected to the Earth, we are processing more feeling in the body. Anything which generates feeling in the body can contribute to grounding. Hatha Yoga, body wiping, sensing the biomagnetism of the earth with our hands and feet, all contribute to grounding. In a tense situation, you may not have time to do yoga postures. In that case, just breathe from the abdomen, remembering feet on ground - Earth and sky. From the center, you can connect with the elements and expand. Remembering the opportunity to heal, the Divine Intent, can help with breathing and grounding.

Processing Feeling/Sensory Orientation

Everyone and everything can be experienced as sensations within the body. With proper breathing and centeredness, we can soften the gaze inward, and feel everything inside, without pushing away discomfort or clinging to comfort. We can allow the moment to move through us. Remembering Divine Intent, allowing breath and grounding, processing our own weakness, turning the eyes inward, looking into the bodyspace, can all contribute to allowing the moment to happen and seeing the true root of the conflict. With conflict comes opportunity.

Facing ourselves

When we resent a person or situation for attacking us, we create a pole that they can grab onto. Through this pole, we are giving our power away to the person or situation. Then we become drained. It's important to focus on what WE need to change. Then, no power leaves our body. Instead, a flood of insights often come to us that otherwise would not bubble up to the surface.

Assertiveness is ok, if it comes from the center, without a desire to make the other wrong or to appear strong. In a passive/aggressive pattern, we have two poles that perpetuate each other. It's important to express our true feelings in the moment. We must work on all levels, not just on some supposed deeper level. We're multidimensional. When anger comes up, sometimes the only way to release it is to express it. If we express it with a desire to hurt, it only perpetuates the polarization.

One time, I was at the (Prescott, AZ) courthouse square. Before entering the bathroom, I twisted out a cigarette and threw it into the garbage can. It was a good and thorough squeeze. However, the security guard followed me into the bathroom, and he got very feisty. I allowed the experience to move through me. Then I spoke my case in one sentence, and let it go, while checking the trash can for smoke, not caring whether he understood my position or not.

When I was resentful of the situation, I felt very drained. Once I turned my attention to what he was really poking at, then no power left my body. I was filled again. The issue was mindfulness, even though I was mindful of completely twisting out the cigarette. I was very spacey at the time.

Sometimes, when someone is watching you like a hawk, waiting for you to screw up, it is easy to lose consciousness and screw up. It doesn't matter. That process could have been prevented through mindfulness. I wasn't being mindful.

The changing of perspective brought a rush of energy and insight. The experience became empowering rather than disempowering.

Almost every time I was kicked off onramps for hitchhiking, I was headed the wrong way anyway. There was something within those officers - an intent within the intent - that truly wanted to help. If I had gotten stuck in resentment in those situations, then I would have missed critical insights into what I should have done that would have been more in alignment with the higher purpose of the situation. Listening is the key. Relaxing into the flow is the key to listening.

If an authority figure abuses his/her power, then, as long as it comes from the core, with recognition of the soul, the true self, then corrective action is appropriate. As mentioned earlier, it's important to work on all levels.

Become Space/Mirroring/Matching the Energy

Spaciousness is love. Love is spaciousness. Anything that's out of balance is neutralized by spaciousness – the all-seeing eye (as opposed to its evil twin – Big Brother). Where there is imbalance, there is a fiercely vibrating polarization. Spaciousness neutralizes that.

Clinging to comfort and pushing away discomfort restricts space, just like restricted breath. Then, we're jumping from pole to pole. It doesn't neutralize anything. It only perpetuates the imbalance. The soul is seeking wholeness. Why not align ourselves with our true Self – the authentic connection to the All or the "One"?

When we truly click with another person, sometimes we do the same things at the same time, speak the same words, etc. We feel truly present with such a person. We can learn this process with friend and foe alike by remembering what such a process feels like. That is what it means to match the energy. It is also taught in some of the martial arts, too. Matching the energy is essential to the mirroring process. Matching is different from repulsion and reaction. Reactions also mirror the energy. However, it is in such a way that perpetuates rather than neutralizes the imbalanced energy.

Avoiding Attack – Prevention

To speak of ways of avoiding attack, it is important to speak of ways we invite attack. If we hold an attitude of being surrounded by idiots who need correction, then naturally we're going to invite challengers. Even if the attitude is not expressed outwardly, it still emanates from within, vibrating outward into our environment, like ripples in a pond, creating poles, which, like a magnet, attract the appropriate corresponding poles to soften the disturbance and bring it into balance. This is one explanation of the principle of Cause and Effect, or Karma.

If we lack self compassion, compassion for ourselves and our own weaknesses, sometimes this is reflected in our environment, in other people. People enter our field whom may be especially hard on us – uncompassionate.

When we're willing to face ourselves compassionately, then there is less need for others to try to soften us.

Some people chant for protection. Every tradition has chants. A deity is some aspect of our true selves, our souls. The symbol is a face of Divinity. The key is LSD – Love, Surrender, Devotion – ever softening, ever deepening. Some gospel singers understand this concept very well. LSD takes us beyond the symbol to that which is beyond form - pure love and spaciousness. It's important to feel it vibrate in your body, gradually making its way down at least to the lower belly, if not further. Allow the eyes to turn inward.

Some people call on Jesus or Angels. Some visualize themselves in the eye of a storm, the safe center of the storm. Then they set an intent, through prayer, for protection from all disharmonic elements that don't serve the highest good. This is followed by visualizing themselves surrounded and permeated by the protective pure white light of the Beloved.

Everyday Practice

We can practice all these principles in peaceful situations. Sometimes, when in the presence of someone who is relaxed and peaceful, that light shines within us. If we're not peaceful in that moment, then feelings come up in the body. Whatever is not peaceful within us bubbles up to the surface. We must learn to process that so that we can match the person's peaceful energy.

Everyone is clear where someone else is weak. This makes us all teachers and students. Processing whatever is triggered within us gives us the first clue to what it is we must learn from another.

All the principles mentioned today contribute to centeredness. Centeredness is the key to knowing exactly how to respond authentically in each moment. The more we practice it in peaceful situations, the better we can do so in tense situations.

Spiritual Practice

A solid spiritual practice is certainly recommended and helps us to improve on all of this stuff. Some people connect to that which is beyond form by connecting with nature, some by running, some by stretching, some by devotion to Jesus, some through energy and some through song. It's important to find our portal and to develop a corresponding practice. A warm up on all levels – muscles, nature, intellect, emotion, energy, imagination, breath, etc. is recommended.

A good method to see that you're entering the right zone is to be mindful of biomagnetism sensitivity, light in forehead, eyes turned inward, nerve energy relaxed and smooth, deeper breath, tendency toward good posture.

When you're finished, engage in your favorite meditation practice. Meditation becomes more natural in this way.

Ok. I'm done talking. Discussion?

Afterward

The most common response to this material is that it seems idealistic to the point that it is nonpracticable. None of us, except true saints, are perfectly present in each moment. Perfectionism can only hinder.

The above-mentioned techniques are practicable and, with practice, will lead to greater presence and therefore greater authenticity of action. In other words, they will lead to more freedom, or to a larger range of options, in each moment. Practice is the key. With consistency, a series of mini-revolutions will add up to major shifts.

Be ready to face and embrace anything that surfaces into consciousness, especially emotions which were previously buried and suppressed.

Some folks are highly sensitive and easily overwhelmed. Perhaps they are processing more than is normal in each moment. More often than not, there is a grounding issue. Grounding exercises and finding ways to generate feeling in the body will gradually take care of this issue. The author has issues of this type himself. Through proper, consistent grounding exercises, the symptoms of overwhelm vanish. Keep a good momentum and the process will continue to build.

Grounding Exercise

Begin with a self massage. Continue with stretching, especially if there is a part of the body that is asking you to stretch it. Breathe into the stretch for at least three breaths.

Relax. Take a few deep breaths. Close your eyes. Be aware of your body from top to bottom. Shift your awareness to the Earth, no matter how high above the ground you are. Remain aware of the body. Be mindful of the Earth's crust and each succeeding layer, all the way to the core.

With feet on ground, establish a connection from the base of your spine all the way to the core of the earth. You can also grow roots from your spine. Relax into it. The Earth is a living and responsive being.

Drain out any foreign tension you may have absorbed throughout the day. Let it drain, through the cord that you created, into the Earth.

Then, let the energy of the Earth rise into your body, nourishing every system in your bodymind. Remember to breathe with the abdomen.

For the rhythmic souls out there, imagine a rhythm or drumbeat in the core of the Earth. Find a similar rhythm in your own body and connect with the core of the Earth. Kinesthetic souls can imagine a pulsation in place of the drumbeat.

Being Present With People

When you are around people, you can begin with centered, abdominal breathing, feeling the abdomen as it gently massages the spine and pelvic floor. Relax and feel the person(s) inside of your body. The only place they exist is within.

Remember the Earth. Even if under pavement, it still exists. Remember the Sky. Relax into both. Then, do the same with the feeling of Wind and Sun. Listen for natural sounds, like a rushing creek, the wind in the trees, crickets or cicadas. Relax with the person(s). Breathe into any uncomfortable sensation.

Your field will expand into space, embracing more and more of the environmental field. Events which were previously overwhelming - taking up a greater percentage of consciousness - will become a smaller fraction of your total experience, and therefore more easily processed. Accepting them into yourself will become easier.

Preparation for Meditation

It all starts with breath. Some say to breathe deeply with the abdomen. Some say to start with where you're at and just breathe consciously. In the second approach, the breath gradually becomes deeper as mindfulness develops without effort. Whatever works for you.

The golden rule is to relax into every exercise, releasing tension and allowing experience to deepen. Love God, the Soul, Universe, the Beloved, The Great Mother, with every breath.

Find a favorite spot in nature, even if it is a flower garden, and relax into the environment. Scan the Earth with your palms and feel the biomagnetism. Soften the palms with each movement.

Give yourself a massage, then stretch. Breathe into it. Play your favorite music that takes you to a deep place within. Read your favorite spiritual text. Sing your favorite chants.

Find a short practice for each level - muscles, emotions, breath, energy, imagination, intellect, breath. Put it all together. Create a routine. Then, if you have a meditation or prayer practice, do it afterward. It will be so much more natural.

Develop a five minute intertwine throughout the day. Little acts, interwoven throughout the day, which deepen presence, go a long way. Most of the work will occur behind the scenes. The effects you notice are only the tip of the iceberg. Trust that there is a much greater process occurring than what you are aware of.

Accept whatever bubbles up into consciousness as stuck energy loosens. It's the only way to heal.

Presence is spaciousness. Spaciousness is Love - the highest reality - the only form of true knowledge.

Support this service by purchasing a paperback copy and the audio course at www.DeeperMeditation.net

Purchase the Deeper Meditation Audio Course and receive a free paperback copy of this book shipped to you anywhere in the world.

Ask about the employee wellness program package featuring the audio course, corporate employee trainings with Tom Von Deck and a secular and wellness oriented edition of this book.

And tell all your friends that they can take this course at www.DeeperMeditation.net

Suggestions for Further Reading

One of the closest things that comes to mind is the writings of William Martino, founder of the Flow Program, Kung Fu master, meditation master and former monk of the Zen and Vedic traditions. His writings are nothing like this one. They are, however, a great complement to this literature and contain some of the same ideas with varying emphasis.

You'll learn how to access your inner peace in this very moment and what physiological signs to look for while you're doing this.

William's free instruction ebooks are organized like ecstatic poetry – that is, not at all. You will find many gems therein that will provoke startling "ah-ha's" within you.

William's writings can be found at www.WilliamMartino.com. If the link becomes obsolete, then search for him in a search engine.

For information related to the Appendix, see Transforming Conflict into Harmony by Khor Chu Cheng. If you're lucky, the book is still free at www.scribd.com/meiskhor

Made in the USA
Lexington, KY
06 May 2012